It's the White Fox

Loyalty Passion and Creativity

Written By

Dr. Alex

Contents

Summary

No man will ever set foot in the always-western Manless Land where the Pale Fox prowls.

There is no fear in the Pale Fox's hunting grounds, the Manless Land of the eternal west. Notail, a fox born without a tail in the stone forest, has no choice but to leave his home and start over somewhere else. He plans to go to the west in search of the mythical manless realm of the Pale Fox.

But the Black Dog is after him, and Notail has little reason to have faith. He has no choice but to keep heading west. Don't stop your westward progress. Hold on to your fantasies of the Manless Land and the Pale Fox...

Chapter 1: Without its tail, a fox is just another animal

They dubbed him Notail since he was a fox born without a tail. As he prowled the stone forest, the first snowflakes of winter began to fall.

After walking on the rough stone of the main tracks below, his paws found the snow to be a great relief. As he did so, he took a deep breath of the atmosphere. For him, this was the whole universe. Every detail was familiar to him. It was a path he'd been walking on for his whole life. He blended into the background like a sleek shadow, undetected.

The regulations set down by his father were strictly adhered to. When Notail was a young cub, his father informed him, "You need the rules more than any other fox."

Notail had understood his dad's meaning even back then. His tail was missing. To put it bluntly, he was peculiar. Incomplete. He needed all the aid he could receive if he was going to mature into a real fox, if he was going to learn to hunt, and if he was going to be able to provide for a mate and pups.

On the other hand, Notail was completely independent at this point. He went hunting in his spare time. Only a fleeting sight of him remained before he disappeared completely.

Never go on a daytime hunt. As rules go, that one was quite straightforward. In the daytime, hunting was very difficult. Too many troop transports. Far too many male gazes. There wasn't enough scavenged man food sitting around unattended. We need more rats. There are no concealed spaces to sneak around in.

He casually strolled out into the night. From his secret cave, he followed the line of trees that surrounded the open area until he reached the home of the fire-changed fowl. For a time he hid out in the bushes and observed his surroundings.

Far off, he could make out the screams of approaching man carriers. This music pushed you.

Someone wobbling and staggering in front of him caught his attention. That guy's chugging down the noxious water. The man was yelling at the night sky. Notail cast his gaze towards the moon. Although the moon was visible tonight, it was quickly obscured by a thick layer of snow clouds. His eyes returned to the guy, and he shook his head. The idea occurred to him, "What idiots man was, man expects all the world to listen." A fox without a tail would have known that the moon never responds.

As the man's voice gradually weakened, he died. Yes, this was the last straw. It was Notail's turn to take center stage. He was sensitive to even the faintest sounds. a displaced bird squabbling in the bushes. Any rodent that ventures down to sniff about the tunnels. Every self-aggrandizing cat licking its chin and purring blissfully. As he narrowed his attention on his prey, manmade sounds receded into the distance. There was a corresponding improvement in the cleanliness of the aromas. He had a clearer whiff of the location of the fire-changed chicken. He felt drawn to it. For guidance, he turned his attention there. It was late, and there was no one around. As he did so, he shook his head.

To get what you need, you need to go hunting first. That regulation had always bothered him.

You could ask, "But isn't scavenging hunting?" Earlier, he had questioned his dad.

Before the night his father took him to the spot where man fire changed fowl, all his father would say was, "Hunt first, locate true food before you turn to man food." He was tempted by the aroma of cooking chicken, but his father had him stand in the bushes and watch while strangers arrived and carried the birds away. Slowly, when his father urged him to follow, they made their way down a shadow track until they arrived. Chickens that were just tossed out. Abandoned. Not cold yet. Delicious. Not all went to get one, but his dad stopped him.

A resounding "No" had sprung from his lips. You should take this as a lesson. When we can't go hunting, we resort to scavenging.

The previous night, Notail had dreamt about cozy hens roasting over an open fire. A sensation of biting into crisp skin and tender meat. For a guy to have one all to himself.

To Notail, it was obvious that his dad was mistaken. To scavenge, locate the appropriate areas, evade man, and beat other foxes to the prize pickings required as much expertise as hunting a rat.

He walked off along a manmade path with his back to us.

Keeping low, he followed mandates along the shadowy path. The vacant guy's food was overflowing and almost spoiled when he arrived. Lots of it existed. The meal was delicious. He'd have enough to eat. In case his search was unsuccessful, he always made a note of the locations. His face lit up at the prospect. He never missed a hunt because of it.

Inside the stone jungle, he continued to advance. Even when the temperature outside dropped, he remained unfazed. He was listening to the noises too intently. He froze at the sound of a door slamming shut. He skulked up against the stone edge while murmurs from men waited for him. He overheard two cats screaming at each other to the exclusion of all other noises. As they fought, he observed. He reasoned, "Perhaps I can go after the loser." However, there was no victor. There was a brief lull in the combat, and Notail continued past the dozing man carriers.

In time, he reached a broad main track. A native of this area, he was well familiar with it. They were in a perilous area. He kept his eye on the man-made path. Outside of it was a vast landscape of maidens separated by open areas and teeming with wild rabbits. He sometimes went hunting there and would find rabbits sleeping it off on a grassy hillside. The area was a hunter's paradise.

Giant people movers rumbled down the man track. Even though they were man-carrying foxes, he was too swift for them. One of his dad's commandments was "never loiter on the main tracks," which meant always moving quickly. Notail had seen many of the foxes he knew die in the man tracks of the stone forest. When Notail went out in search of game, he often came upon their mangled remains strewn over the ground or pressed up against stone walls. Broken. Ignored by humans and allowed to deteriorate or be eaten.

He bolted as a second-man transporter screamed by. More were coming, but he was going too quickly to catch them. To put it simply, they wouldn't squish him. Their lights were as intense as the sun in the morning, and he could feel them searing at him, yet he was unafraid. There was no longer any trace of their commotion once he had taken off running.

Leaving the man track behind, he padded up to a large man. Inside, he heard men talking. As he observed their shadows, he realized that they were laughing. He continued his wandering while his tummy growled.

On the weird manden where people knelt, he saw a roost of crows sitting on its highest point. It was clear he was keeping an eye on them. They kept an eye on him and knew he was helpless against them in a hunt. His father constantly warned him that crow flesh is rough and unpleasant.

When one of them yelled "Dark," he knew it was them.

Dark, said the second crow in response.

One by one, they started calling. There was just that one word repeated endlessly. It's dark, dark, and dark.

At this point, the moon was out of sight. They were correct; it was rather gloomy outside. A pervasive gloom that appeared incapable of ever dissipating from the global landscape. He scoffed at the birds, thinking that this was how the earth usually looked at night, with daylight always following.

This time, Notail didn't stick around. He padded through an orderly row of artificial trees and onto a patch of white grass. A massive manden stood before him. Smoke rose softly from the manden, carrying the aroma of cooking meat, and he could feel the warmth from inside.

As he approached the man, he gave a sniff and padded over. Dogs and cats were completely undetectable to him. No sleepy bunnies could be found. The aroma of hot man food alone is enough to tempt anybody.

Never accept food from a human's hands. If he broke that rule, Notail frequently thought, his life would be so much simpler. In the stone forest, there once lived a lady who cared for foxes by providing them with food. It wasn't the first time he'd seen foxes eat out of her palm. Take a lick out of her palm. Akin to dogs, at best. He foxed around.

He stooped next to the stone edge of the manden and peered inside. The lady held the man-cub in her arms. The infant human was brand new. She clutched the bare creature to her bosom. It nursed off of her. Its eyes were shut tight. In other words, it was happy. While his hunger grumbled, he watched the man-cub eat.

One thing his father had drilled into his head was a rule he was to never forget.

Don't ever harm humankind's young.

His dad always drilled into him that the family was foxes. All of this is man's world: the enormous rhinestone cliffs of light and stillness; the black shadow tracks; the den in which you sleep each night; the undertracks underneath us; the main tracks. Foxes are prey animals, and if they harm a human, people will kill them. The day a fox wounds a man's cub is the day they will hunt us down and kill us all. Even if you went a year without eating, son, you still shouldn't injure them.

Notail was aware that some foxes did not follow his father's ways. Foxes mostly depend on scraps and garbage cans for sustenance. sluggish foxes that no longer feared humans carrying food. However, he had never heard of foxes harming human youngsters. The

foxes that ate off people's hands never disregarded that regulation.
The human cub was laid down by its mother. That, she wrapped up. It seemed to be a comfortable temperature. Again, Notail disregarded the rumblings of his stomach.

He remained to keep an eye on the manden. Even though the night was becoming cooler, the location gave off the impression that it was rather comfortable.

He then saw a guy bend down and nuzzle the cub beside the mom. No tail shivered. The snow had collected around his spine. He just brushed it off. As the guy and lady cuddled, he observed. There was a rumble in his tummy.

The cub's sleeping area was made darker by the father and the lady. As they continued through their manden, he finally came across it. A beginning. Lightly cracked. He turned his attention to the couple. They hadn't even noticed he was there; they were too busy eating.

As he got nearer to the door, he stepped inside. However, neither the guy nor the lady seemed to have heard him. Move in here, just a little bit. He could almost make out his dad's voice warning him away from the manden. But unlike Notail, his dad wasn't sneaky and quiet. They never would have found out where he came from if his dad hadn't been careful. On the other hand, the manden itself was a comfortable place to be. The temperature of his paws was uncomfortably low. The maiden's warmth was permeating his skin. He felt confident sneaking inside and basking in the warmth without being seen. For the time being.

He'd gotten near enough to the crack to overhear the guy and lady conversing. The security of their odd-man words was ensured. Nothing could harm men. Where was their cause for alarm? They knew their youngster was toasty and secure, so they joked and ate and were generally in good spirits.

They dubbed him Notail since he was a fox born without a tail.

As he prowled the stone forest, the first snowflakes of winter began to fall.

After walking on the rough stone of the man tracks below, his paws found the snow to be a great relief. As he did so, he took a deep breath of the atmosphere. For him, this was the whole universe. Every detail was familiar to him. It was a path he'd been walking on for his whole life. He blended into the background like a sleek shadow, undetected.

The regulations set down by his father were strictly adhered to.

When Notail was a young cub, his father informed him, "You need the rules more than any other fox." Notail had understood his dad's meaning even back then. His tail was missing. To put it bluntly, he was peculiar. Incomplete. He needed all the aid he could receive if he was going to mature into a real fox, if he was going to learn to hunt, and if he was going to be able to provide for a mate and pups.

On the other hand, Notail was completely independent at this point. He went hunting in his spare time. Only a fleeting sight of him remained before he disappeared completely.

Never go on a daytime hunt. As rules go, that one was quite straightforward. In the daytime, hunting was very difficult. Too many troop transports. Far too many male gazes. There wasn't enough scavenged man food sitting around unattended. We need more rats. There are no concealed spaces to sneak around in.

He casually strolled out into the night. From his secret cave, he followed the line of trees that surrounded the open area until he reached the home of the fire-changed fowl. For a time he hid out in the bushes and observed his surroundings.

Far off, he could make out the screams of approaching man carriers. This music pushed you.

Someone wobbling and staggering in front of him caught his attention. That guy's chugging down the noxious water. The man was yelling at the night sky. Notail cast his gaze towards the moon. Although the moon was visible tonight, it was quickly obscured by a thick layer of snow clouds. His eyes returned to the guy, and he shook his head. The idea occurred to him, "What idiots man was, man expects all the world to listen." A fox without a tail would have known that the moon never responds.

As the man's voice gradually weakened, he died. Yes, this was the last straw. It was Notail's turn to take center stage. He was sensitive to even the faintest sounds. a displaced bird squabbling in the bushes. Any rodent that ventures down to sniff about the tunnels. Every self-aggrandizing cat licking its chin and purring blissfully. As he narrowed his attention on his prey, manmade sounds receded into the distance. There was a corresponding improvement in the cleanliness of the aromas. He had a clearer whiff of the location of the fire-changed chicken. He felt drawn to it. For guidance, he turned his attention there. It was late, and there was no one around. As he did so, he shook his head.

To get what you need, you need to go hunting first. That regulation had always bothered him.

You could ask, "But isn't scavenging hunting?" Earlier, he had questioned his dad.

Before the night his father took him to the spot where man fire changed fowl, all his father would say was, "Hunt first, locate true food before you turn to man food." He was tempted by the aroma of cooking chicken, but his father had him stand in the bushes and watch while strangers arrived and carried the birds away. Slowly, when his father urged him to follow, they made their way down a shadow track until they arrived. Chickens that were just tossed out. Abandoned. Not cold yet. Delicious. Not all went to get one, but his dad stopped him.

A resounding "No" had sprung from his lips. You should take this as a lesson. When we can't go hunting, we resort to scavenging.

The previous night, Notail had dreamt about cozy hens roasting over an open fire. A sensation of biting into crisp skin and tender meat. For a guy to have one all to himself.

To Notail, it was obvious that his dad was mistaken. To scavenge, locate the appropriate areas, evade man, and beat other foxes to the prize pickings required as much expertise as hunting a rat.

He walked off along a manmade path with his back to us.

Keeping low, he followed maidens along the shadowy path. The vacant guy's food was overflowing and almost spoiled when he arrived. Lots of it existed. The meal was delicious. He'd have enough to eat. In case his search was unsuccessful, he always made a note of the locations. His face lit up at the prospect. He never missed a hunt because of it.

Inside the stone jungle, he continued to advance. Even when the temperature outside dropped, he remained unfazed. He was listening to the noises too intently. He froze at the sound of a door slamming shut. He skulked up against the stone edge while murmurs from men waited for him. He overheard two cats screaming at each other to the exclusion of all other noises. As they fought, he observed. He reasoned, "Perhaps I can go after the loser." However, there was no victor. There was a brief lull in the combat, and Notail continued on past the dozing man carriers.

In time, he reached a broad man track. A native of this area, he was well familiar with it. They were in a perilous area. He kept his eye on the man-made path.

Outside of it was a vast landscape of maidens separated by open areas and teeming with wild rabbits. He sometimes went hunting there and would find rabbits sleeping it off on a grassy hillside. The area was a hunter's paradise.

Giant people movers rumbled down the man track. Even though they were man-carrying foxes, he was too swift for them. One of his dad's commandments was "never loiter on the man tracks," which meant always moving quickly. Notail had seen many of the foxes he knew die in the man tracks of the stone forest. When Notail went out in search of game, he often came upon their mangled remains strewn over the ground or pressed up against stone walls. Broken. Ignored by humans and allowed to deteriorate or be eaten.

He bolted as a second-man transporter screamed by. More were coming, but he was going too quickly to catch them. To put it simply, they wouldn't squish him. Their lights were as intense as the sun in the morning, and he could feel them searing at him, yet he was unafraid. There was no longer any trace of their commotion once he had taken off running.

Leaving the man track behind, he padded up to a large man. Inside, he heard men talking. As he observed their shadows, he realized that they were laughing. He continued his wandering while his tummy growled.

On the weird manden where people knelt, he saw a roost of crows sitting on its highest point. It was clear he was keeping an eye on them. They kept an eye on him and knew he was helpless against them in a hunt. His father constantly warned him that crow flesh is rough and unpleasant.
When one of them yelled "Dark," he knew it was them.

Dark, said the second crow in response.

One by one, they started calling. There was just that one word repeated endlessly. It's dark, dark, and dark. At this point, the moon was out of sight. They were correct; it was rather gloomy outside. A pervasive gloom that appeared incapable of ever dissipating from the global landscape. He scoffed at the birds, thinking that this was how the earth usually looked at night, with daylight always following.

This time, Notail didn't stick around. He padded through an orderly row of artificial trees and onto a patch of white grass. A massive manden stood before him. Smoke rose softly from the manden, carrying the aroma of cooking meat, and he could feel the warmth from inside.

As he approached the man, he gave a sniff and padded over. Dogs and cats were completely undetectable to him. No sleepy bunnies could be found. The aroma of hot man food alone is enough to tempt anybody.

Never accept food from a human's hands. If he broke that rule, Notail frequently thought, his life would be so much simpler. In the stone forest, there once lived a lady who cared for foxes by providing them with food. It wasn't the first time he'd seen foxes eat out of her palm. Take a lick out of her palm. Akin to dogs, at best. He foxed around.

He stooped next to the stone edge of the manden and peered inside. The lady held the man-cub in her arms. The infant human was brand new. She clutched the bare creature to her bosom. It nursed off of her. Its eyes were shut tight. In other words, it was happy. While his hunger grumbled, he watched the man-cub eat.

One thing his father had drilled into his head was a rule he was to never forget.

Don't ever harm humankind's young.

His dad always drilled into him that the family was foxes. All of this is man's world: the enormous rhinestone cliffs of light and stillness; the black shadow tracks; the den in which you sleep each night; the undertracks underneath us; the man tracks. Foxes are prey animals, and if they harm a human, people will kill them. The day a fox wounds a man's cub is the day they will hunt us down and kill us all. Even if you went a year without eating, son, you still shouldn't injure them.

Notail was aware that some foxes did not follow his father's ways. Foxes mostly depend on scraps and garbage cans for sustenance. sluggish foxes that no longer feared humans carrying food. However, he had never heard of foxes harming human youngsters. The foxes that ate off people's hands never disregarded that regulation.
The human cub was laid down by its mother. That, she wrapped up. It seemed to be a comfortable temperature. Again, Notail disregarded the rumblings of his stomach.

He remained to keep an eye on the manden. Even though the night was becoming cooler, the location gave off the impression that it was rather comfortable.

He then saw a guy bend down and nuzzle the cub beside the mom. No tail shivered. The snow had collected around his spine. He just brushed it off. As the guy and lady cuddled, he observed. There was a rumble in his tummy.

The cub's sleeping area was made darker by the father and the lady. As they continued through their manden, he finally came across it. A beginning. Lightly cracked. He turned his attention to the couple. They hadn't even noticed he was there; they were too busy eating.

As he got nearer to the door, he stepped inside. However, neither the guy nor the lady seemed to have heard him. Move in here, just a little bit. He could almost make out his dad's voice warning him away from the manden. But unlike Notail, his dad wasn't sneaky and quiet. They never would have found out where he came from if his dad hadn't been careful. On the other hand, the manden itself was a really comfortable place to be. The temperature of his paws was uncomfortably low. The maiden's warmth was permeating his skin. He felt confident sneaking inside and basking in the warmth without being seen. For the time being.

He'd gotten near enough to the crack to overhear the guy and lady conversing. The security of their odd-man words was ensured. Obviously, nothing could harm men. Where was their cause for alarm? They knew their youngster was toasty and secure, so they joked and ate and were generally in good spirits.

Chapter 2: Guarantee of Sustenance

She walked up to him and nuzzled his neck. He kindly let go of the bunny for her to catch.

His little ones were tumbling about and biting each other's tails as they played. Before he could even get a word out, they had both sprinted up to him, with one sitting on his back and the other nibbling toothlessly at his leg.

According to his partner, "don't get them enthusiastic;" they are exhausted.

As the cub leaped from his back, Notail stooped low.

The thought of hunting had crossed his mind, and he mused, "Perhaps I might capture a delicious cub or two."

The youngsters aped his squatting position.

Slowly, Notail approached. The cubs also advanced.

His companion warned, "They could devour you before you eat them."
The man let out a chuckle.

The best hunter in the stone jungle is me, he boasted. As if two cub scouts could defeat me.

The youngsters made a barking noise and jumped forward.

It hurt, he yelled, and he and the cubs rolled about on the ground. As the song goes, "They chased me, they hunted me!"

The two of them had a jovial exchange. Two of the cubs became angry and bit at him. He imagined that one day they might prove to be adept hunters.

As he slept, he propped his paws up in the air.

I'm giving up, he said. "Congratulations, you're the winner."

He delivered his cubs mulched chunks of rabbit that his mate had chewed up for them to eat. At that point, they both leaned forward and rested their heads on his shoulder. Their fluffy tails brushed on his fur, and he smiled. Some foxes, including his siblings, had warned him that he would never find a mate or father any children due to his missing tail. But he had a partner and fathered two healthy cubs with flawless tails, which were ahead of his siblings. He took a glance at his flawless cubs.

The cubs eventually went to sleep. After scarfing down some rabbit, Notail slept down as well.

Before he had cubs, all he could think about was his cave. His partner came first. Just an awful dream. An empty dream. For those who feel alone.

His partner awakened him by pressing her nose on his. There had been very little sleep for him. Night had not yet been driven gone by the dawn.

She predicted, "They'll be hungry again shortly."

Carefully, he got to his feet, and she joined him next to the cubs.

He went outdoors and glanced around. The stone forest was awakening and snow was falling.

It's a lot of weight, he said.

In response, she gave a little nod.

Furthermore, "it's falling early," she said.

He could read the terror on her face. She was thinking something, and he was able to read her mind. It was not a good idea to have cubs during the winter. Cubs have to work hard to get food. It won't work that way for Notail. Even if the globe was frozen over, he was certain he could get them food.

He nuzzled her and assured her, "I will find sufficient for us all." I tracked out a chubby hare for us to eat. A rabbit a night till we have fire-changed chicks.

She responded, "I know you will," and then she blinked her eyes shut. However, the weather is supposed to become quite chilly very soon.

He nuzzled her.

After he assured her that he would locate food for them, she beamed.

There, Notail kept an eye on his pups and his wife. To put it simply, they had fallen asleep. Now that autumn was giving way to winter, they slept a lot. He could see the world beyond the white curtain that had been drawn over it. The room was suddenly hit by a blast of cold air. He lay down in silence next to them. He foxed around. They would never go hungry in his presence.

However, time passed, snow fell, and temperatures dropped to record lows.

The cubs hadn't eaten for five days.

The cold of winter was suffocating everything. The stone forest was hidden from view by a blanket of snow. It stifled any possibility of scavenging and drove the rabbits and rodents into a profound slumber.

Truly, he was an idiot. It was difficult for foxes to hunt throughout the winter, and much more difficult for them to give birth.

His father once advised him, to the amusement of his siblings, "If you're fortunate and you find yourself a partner, make sure your cubs arrive in summer. The summer season is a wonderful time to have cubs. An Abundance of Food."

Unfortunately for him, his partner never settled down with any kind of family. Too much of her life had been spent on her own. He hoped more than everything that she would never have to be lonely again.

She told him a long time ago, “We should have two cubs.” Two tiny Details would be perfect.

He assured her, "They'll have tails," and she chuckled.

Not having a tail seems OK to me. Look at us, she remarked with a grin, "we don't have one and we're quite content without one. She often made fun of his

insecurity about his missing tail. She had even assured him that she would fashion him a brand new one out of the foliage. She promised him that she would always have new flowers to weave into it.
Again he repeated, "They will have tails," and this time she chuckled.

"As long as they have us, those foxes will be the happiest in the world," she said.

When the cubs finally arrived, everyone was overjoyed. Up to this point, that is. At least, until the onset of winter coincided with their arrival. Until the onset of winter left them famished.

His wife cried the first night he returned home hungry.

I can't afford to lose them," she pleaded.

They suckled on her, savoring her last drops of milk, but she continued to wail despite his efforts to comfort her.

She told him, "You don't know what it is like to not have a family."

There was some truth to what she said. No, he didn't do it. He had his parents and brothers always available to him. She had always been a solitary fox.

No parents, no family, no one to call dad or mom. He was shocked to see her among the daisies beside the lake since he had never seen a fox so skinny before. Despite this, her beauty was undeniable.

She hid among the flowers that day, but after his return the following days she joined him there. After they had a meal by the lake, he knew they would be together forever.

There was no way he could let her down now. This, he would not do.

At his cubs, he cast his gaze. To put it simply, they had fallen asleep. The lack of food was the cause of their nap. A cub could sleep indefinitely if it were starving like that.

"Maybe we could sleep till the snow melts if you could get us something, anything," she pleaded. We only need one successful hunt to provide us with enough food for the winter. Keep your word and come up with something.

Another vow he had made to his partner in the past resurfaced in his mind.

When they first met, he had promised to protect her at any cost. Considering his age at the time, it was a foolish pledge.

His heart wrenched at the remembrance. He had gone out night after night without any success. Every night he would visit the location where the hens were transformed by fire, but it was to no use. There was no discarded man food to be found in the shadow tracks. The globe has been frozen solid.

But he was out hunting tonight, and he was going to bring home a tasty treat for them. Foraging for himself, he would succeed. He would go on killing sprees and feed his cubs the fresh meat. As a group, they lacked strength. They were hungry. Any kind of food. They need a fortifying agent. If the true food was scarce, he would resort to foraging for it. What was important was that he locate food, and he would.

Still, his partner murmured nothing in response to his nuzzling. Like the cubs, she was helpless and frail. She seemed to be asleep with her eyes closed. She was simply isolating herself more. There was nothing she could do except hope.

As he did, he nuzzled her cheek.

I guarantee it," he said.

He came sauntering out into the cold night from his cave. One snow-laden branch he pushed aside. Flakes of ice landed on his fur.

Chapter 3: What's New in the Ruins

It was peaceful in the stone forest. There were no signs of human activity in the manmade pathways. It seems that even man was content to remain in his mandates, where he could enjoy the warmth and plenty of food. Not going hunting was not necessary, he said with a grin.

Walking up man track after main track, constantly inhaling the air. Frost covered the stone forest's aromas. Hidden. Lost. Even the scent of the undertracks was too faint for him to detect. He sloshed through the bleak slush, his paws numb with cold. He saw a skinny mouse scurrying down a dark passageway, but the chill had sapped his stealth ability as well. The rat was scared off by his labored, almost frozen breathing, and it ran away.

The time was too critical to let his partner down.

Further, into the stone jungle, he ascended. The man carriers chugged along the main tracks. A guy slipped and fell on the ice, and he witnessed it all. A man sprang up, massaging his head, and started shouting about nothing in particular. The guy continued stumbling down the man track.

Notail needed to eat. Even though dawn was on its way, the night lingered on.

Going down a dark passage, he discovered a hollow manden. The ash made the air dark. There was evidence of a fire. Its top had caved down partially. His entrance inside the house was delayed. In the ash-covered ground, he detected a bird's aroma. A young, rat-resistant pigeon with a dead end. Fresh and untainted, just as if he'd killed it personally. The freezing temperatures were the last straw. Many creatures had died in the cold, and he had seen it. Even though this pigeon was just a squab and would have been of little use to his offspring, he clung to it since it was true food. He assured himself, "It will give me the strength to go on hunting."

He bit down forcefully on the chook's bones. Bruised and bloody, his nose was. The blood had a pleasant flavor, so he licked it. Even now, there is a small warmth. After shattering the bird's ribcage, he stuck his tongue inside and chewed on its heart. He swallowed pieces of liver and lung. He ate until there was only a sphere of a head with a pair of dark eyes staring up at him. He chewed it well, feeling the fluids, meat, and brain all meld together, before swallowing.

Dark, dark, dark, someone's voice said.

Blood stained the fur around his lips and he glanced up. More pigeons were perched nearby, watching him. There were a lot of them there. There were hundreds of black eyes staring at him. How they came to know the bird was a mystery to him.

Another repetition of "black, dark, dark" echoed from the distance. He had no idea which bird had been communicating with him.

He then yelled back up, "Leave me be, birds." As the saying goes, "I know it's dark, black, and chilly."

Those birds looked down at him with disdain. One hundred icy watches looking on.

A voice said, "Stupid, fool, fool," and one of the pigeons jumped out of its stone nest and into the ash below.

It approached him at a close range. A bobbling motion was made in its head. It swelled up its breast and began scratching at the scorched ground.

His piercing cry reflected off the stones and was repeated by the birds overhead.

A question: "What do you want?" The bird made a loud squawking sound, so Notail snatched at it fast.

He entertained the notion that if he killed it and a couple of the others, they would all make tasty meals.

The bird reversed course and returned. You, fox, it snarled. "You foxes, all of you. Sorry to hear about this.

The pigeons all said it together: "Sorry, sorry, sorry."

The pigeon's tail snapped again, but it only hopped further back.

Why should you feel bad about me? I should be the one feeling terrible for you," he replied. "You're only pigeons; if I wanted to, I could eat any of you.

Shaking its head, the bird made a face.

Dark, dark, dark, it proclaimed. Currently, "You do not know. You have not heard the story yet. You have big fox ears but no hearing ability, therefore you haven't heard anything.

Singing, "Have not heard, have not heard, have not heard," the birds made it clear they had not.

Ignorantly asking, "Not heard what?" It was a question that Notail had. His instinct told him to attack the bird, snap its neck with one bite, and silence it, but he refrained. It's completely dark, completely dark, completely dark. He recalled hearing the cawing of crows.

The bird said, "Bad foxes." Perhaps you have tonight tasted other blood, or perhaps one of your kind has wounded a man's female offspring. There was a deliberate attempt to kill the chick by inflicting fatal injuries. The guy is now furious. All foxes, in his opinion, should be exterminated. He's trying to get rid of you. He has released his canine hunters to track down and kill each one of you.

The birds resumed their chant of "dark, black, dark." You guys, you guys, you guys.

Notail wiped his bloody lips with his paw. He recalled the door being opened and the newborn man's gentle breathing. There was a distinct recollection of his having turned aside. Shaking his head, he dismissed the idea. No, I doubt that any other fox could be that naive. The abandoned manden was greeted by a brisk wind. Perhaps a fox might get desperate during this winter, he reasoned. But, no. It was a silent, gloomy night. To this far, he had not encountered any canines. No unusual odors had reached his nose. He knew the pigeons were mistaken; no cold season could make a fox seem that naive. He pondered the leftover feathers in his dish. By forcing me to eat their buddy, he reasoned, they might make me experience their terror.

He then turned aside, said something, and disappeared into the darkness.

Don't waste your time on a bird's gibberish. His father should have had a rule about it.

The dawn was almost upon us. Man's waking would soon be heard across the stone forest, but his cubs would still go hungry.

He daydreamed about going back to his lair. Sounds like they've started whining again. Their eyes met. He listened to the cries of his hungry cubs. He just couldn't deal with it.

He went down, then up, then down, and so on. Human eyes would never be able to see him. He moved quite quickly. Very dapper, in a stylish way. He disappeared in a flash. As he approached the location of the fire-changed chicken, a grin spread over his face. Nobody could be found. The room was dark and deserted, but he caught a whiff of chicken in the air. He had discovered nothing but dead bodies the night before. The fire-changed chicken would be waiting for him tonight. As he had anticipated, he did. He needed to.

The son thanked his father for his support. He was aware that his father would support his decision to become a scavenger, although his father had not

taken him to the site where fire-changed hens were kept.
His dying father often said, "Better to live a smart scavenger than to die a starving idiot."

We may assume that he is very clever. His cubs and he would be safe from harm.

He crept down the shadow track and hopped over the side of a stone wall to reach the spot where the fire changed hens were kept. It seemed as if he were sniffing the air for something. Chicken aroma lingered on in the background. He dug his nose into a putrid male grub. There was so much wasted and spoiled food that he pawed at the mess. We found chicken parts that smelled awful, including legs and wings. Green food came in slimy strands, and the manifold was hard and unfamiliar. More was what he sought. He was looking for something to eat so he could put his cubs to bed and let them rest until the snow melted.

As he tore through the chaos, he finally found it. It was chilly but didn't have the rancid smell of stale man food. It was the closest he could come to "true food." Completely roasted chicken that has been altered by fire. His mouth was used to raise it. In a word, it weighed a lot. It was so close to his tongue that he could taste it. The fruit's sugary juices slid down his gums. He wanted to eat it all at once but restrained himself. He wasn't cut out for it. Theirs was the intended audience.

Away from the flaming chickens, he scampered. Once he returned home, he would be able to relax while watching his pups and mate enjoy the meal he had prepared for them. And then they'd shut themselves in the cave and forget about the outside world. During the winter, they would cuddle up against one other and wait out the storm. The stone forest would once again be bustling with true food once spring arrived. They'd keep on going.

He heard a distant howl as he fled. He didn't pay much attention to it. It may have just been the morning call of a bird or the wail of a waking man carrier. The lack of concern on his part was obvious.

The initial howl was met by an immediate reply, and soon enough the night was filled with the sound of dogs howling.

He snatched the chicken in his teeth and took off.

The 4th Chapter: A Void Within a Void

When he returned to his lair, he saw that something was awry. The silence was oppressive.

The man drew nearer. He took a deep breath and scented the air. That's not how things should be done. The bird crashed on the floor.

The scent of his mate and pups eluded him. That's not how it should work. He'd left his partner and their pups sleeping in the den, and she'd closed her eyes from hunger.

He entered the room gently.

The room was devoid of any people.

No trace of them remained.

His pups' den had a strong canine odor. Their leaves bed was covered with it. The birds' remarks remained ingrained in his memory. Is anyone reading this?

His goal in padding outdoors was to pick up their smell. Do as it says. Help them out. The fox's smell was faint, and it decreased with each step he went away from his lair. Eventually, the dog's fragrance was all that remained. Massive paw tracks were strewn over the snow, leading out into the stone forest. The man tagged along behind them. He went forward in search of fox footprints but discovered man carrier traces instead, which were quickly buried by a slushy grey tangle of snow. No trace of them remained.

In the end, he padded home. The emptiness of it was unprecedented. Poor light. How frigid.

They were sleeping in the same room when he passed out. When they looked at him, he could see the look in their eyes. Their fluffy coats. The little paws. Their rear ends. The eyes of his partner were open to him. His last impression of them was a sad one, not how things should have been. There was a reverberation of her words in his head. His word cut him deeply.

He remained still because he just couldn't get himself to get up. He might have easily remained put and missed out on everything.

It just couldn't be done. They had a pulse. Naturally, they were. I brought them here, he told himself. The man laid his head down, but he did not fall asleep. The planet woke up. Eventually, everyone and everything stopped moving and rested. When he got up, he knew for sure. There was a deathly dog odor in the air. No trace of them remained.

Hungry, he went outside to get the chicken he had fire-transformed, but it had also vanished.

The grass was as frozen as the sky, and both were white. Condensed snow made the ground hard and icy. The massive paw prints had disappeared. It seemed like a fresh snowfall was starting. There was still living in the world. It may have appeared like any other day, but that was not the case. Without a tail and all by himself, he seemed lost.

Chapter 5: A Rat Eating Old Fox

The senior fox knew Notail's dad back when they were both young foxes.

Notail grew up hearing tales of the fox from his father.

His father had informed him, "There is only one fox I know of that has never genuinely frightened man."

After a long while, Notail let out a gasp.

His dad had smiled up at him from below.

Does it come as a shock to you that I would say that? inquired of his dad. I've figured it out. You probably already know that I have no respect for other humans, yet you still expect me to say that. Fact that I am courageous, and I would risk anything for you.

The joke was on his dad. One of the characters laughed, but it was a mournful sound.

It was his father who had told him, "I'm swift like you, but I'm not bold. The only fox I've ever met with such courage was Hunter.

To introduce him to Hunter, his father accompanied him there. It was the height of summer, and they were stuffed with the bounty his dad had uncovered. When the sun finally sank beyond the rosy horizon, they strolled down man tracks to a spot where humans often left their pups. No fox could ever figure out why humans would abandon their young for a whole day in this massive man. Humankind's offspring would emerge one by one. Singing would fill the air, and little humans would sprint towards the vast manden. They'd go back outdoors later in the day, but they'd never go beyond the stone boundary. It was common for them to run and play, and their voices were never harsh like adult males. The stone forest had not yet eroded the gentleness of their voices.

Perhaps they learn to prepare fox meat, as one of his brothers had joked.

Another sibling said, "Yeah, they like foxes without tails." That means "less cutting."

His father had no idea what the guy was doing bringing their cubs here.

Notail questioned his father, "Will Hunter know?" while the older man chuckled.

His father suggested that maybe Hunter had some insight. But I doubt he gives a hoot.

Hunter was discovered dozing off on a rocky outcropping. The sun has set. Even though the location he slept still smelled of man cubs, it was dark and deserted now. He remained asleep even as they drew near.

"Doesn't he know that guy is going to come after him?" Notail enquired.

His father answered, "I told you." Hunter, on the other hand, "has no phobias."

The fox's head sprung up as Hunter heard his father's voice. When he rose, Notail could see the fox's body was covered in scars and ancient wounds; the fox had grey eyes. His legs were powerful, and his neck was big. Even though he was much bigger than Notail's dad, he welcomed them with a kind grin and a quick leap down the ledge of stones.

For Notail, it was a once-in-a-lifetime kind of night. Hunter led them on a hunt. There were a total of six mice and three rabbits captured. They even managed to capture a young cat that desperately wanted to get away.

With a hasty, "Don't be silly, cat," Hunter abruptly cut off further discussion. As the foxes like to say: "We are foxes and we are hungry."

At first light, Hunter took them to the spot where he first made man tremble.

Under the rounded stone, there was a narrow man track with two entrances. A great man carrier would occasionally pass overhead, causing a clicking rumble. There was a lot of fear in Notail's stomach there. The day had begun, and man would soon be arriving. Human being after human being. There were even dog owners among them. The hounds would scent them, but Notail did his best to keep his courage. To prove his bravery to Hunter.

This is a regular stop for me," Hunter volunteered. I'm hanging around here for the heaviest guy in town to show up. This guy is big. Having a dog along for the hunt makes everything easier, but it's still fun without one. Whenever they get too near to my hiding spot, I come barreling out, snarling and growling, and I snap at them.

Are they something you consume? It was a question that Notail had posed.

Hunter didn't mock him in any way.

A resounding "no" came from the fox. I just terrify them and give pursue until we reach the river. As a rule, they flee. They have to run so fast that even the dogs have to keep up.

When a large guy finally showed up, Hunter delivered as promised. He suddenly sprang from the bushes and charged the scared guy, barking like a crazed fox. The guy was a giant. Rather plump and barrel-chested. But when he saw Hunter, he took off running. He sprinted quicker than anybody expected a fat guy to run, surprising both Notail and Hunter. When Hunter returned, he found Notail and his father still laughing hysterically in the bushes. Notail returned to his burrow and proclaimed himself the world's most courageous fox after he and his companions had had breakfast with the feline.

Currently, Hunter was well into his senior years. He was old and whitened and withered and hardly recognizable from his former self.

At the same outcropping of stone where Notail had first encountered him, he sat there. He had lost a lot of weight and his legs looked like sticks. His neck wasn't strong enough to carry his heavy head. There were several scars all over his body.

When Notail came upon him, he was munching on a rat.

Seeing Notail pad closer, he glanced up. His fur moved nervously as he walked. His frail legs shook just so little. His droopy grey eyes seemed like they were about to burst into tears at any moment.

Hunter continued, his voice trembling with age and anxiety, "Man is hunting again."

Hunter's muzzle had a new cut on it, and it was moist and yellow with infection. He was missing most of his teeth.

That's why they don't want us here," Hunter told Notail. We shouldn't have left the Manless Land in the first place.

Moose Notail needed to eat. With suspicion, he studied the rodent. Hunter was unable to penetrate the rat's bone and reach the sparse marrow within. It was thrown away.

To what facility are foxes removed? It was a question that Notail had to ask.

Hunter's head tilted as his eyes blinked slowly from fatigue.

'They don't take them anyplace,' he replied.

That was something Notail already knew, but seeing Hunter say it put an end to any remaining optimism. No trace of them remained.

Hunter questioned the reasoning of the inquiry.

Notail avoided saying the words. This would be the case if he stated them. This person or group would be well-known.

'Man snatched my mate and cubs,' Notail remarked. "The humans had dogs kill us off. My mate and our pups were killed.

After a moment, Hunter acknowledged with a nod. It's a "dark period," he said. My heart goes out to you, Notail. You need to get out of here right now.

Notail enquired, "And to where?"

Slowly, Hunter raised his head. It seemed like he was exhausted. A door banged shut not too far away, and then I heard a man chuckling. Notail looked around the clearing where the human cubs had arrived, but there was no one else there. The first human infants were still fast asleep.

Hunter returned to observing his rat.

Between chews, he said, "You should discover the Pale Fox."

It was the tales of the Pale Fox that Notail recalled. Where the Pale Fox hunts and there is no fear is the Manless Land, in the eternal west.

The song echoed back to a time when rhymes were common. One might recite this poem aloud on chilly evenings and feel the warmth of the words spread across the earth. It turned out to be an urban legend. A tale for chumps and dummies.

The Pale Fox does not exist, Notail said.

Hunter gave him a long, intense stare. From his nose to his stump of a tail, he examined him thoroughly.

At the long end, Hunter admitted, "You have no tail." I instructed your father to abandon you when you were born because a fox has to be completely mature otherwise he's not a fox at all. I used to believe that a fox born without a tail would be a burden on all foxes because of his deficiencies. Your dad just ignored me. Finally, I get it and can admit he was correct. You have had to be tough, hardy, and swift to survive. While you may be alive right now, staying in the stone forest will lead to your demise just as it has mine and that of my mate and pups.

When asked, Hunter, sighed. He shut his perpetually teary eyes. When he opened them, the fox Notail remembered from long ago seemed less grey.

Hunter's voice was no longer shaky or feeble when he whispered, "Listen to me, Notail." Since you have no other options, you must put your faith in the Pale

Fox. As long as you remain in the stone forest, you will see nothing but night. Sometimes, if I look closely, I can still make out a very weak glow in the distance. When I was younger, I often entertained the idea of venturing beyond the stone forest in pursuit of the Manless Land. I had faith in my abilities and thought I could pull them off. However, I appreciated my stone forest and the terror I instilled in man. Now that I'm elderly, I can't go anyplace, and Mother Vixen constantly nudges and coos at me. I'm drawn to the sound of her kind voice. Oh, Notail, you have no idea what she calls me, but that is just and proper. Still, you are quite young. You should get out of the stone forest, Notail; your life is over here, but it shouldn't be the end of you. Help me track down the White Fox.

A cough came from Hunter. He had crimson fur around his lips.

The fox responded, "You can't stay here with me any longer. I'm sick of talking about it.

Padding off, no tail did. He stood at the edge of the area from whence the first humans emerged, facing west into the remaining night. The Manless Land, according to his father, was out there, where the sun goes to sleep and the water gently murmurs. Places where fear does not exist and man cannot go. Out here in the wild west. All the time heading west.

Chapter 6: The Crawling Darkness

Moving stealthily, Notail followed many tracks he was unfamiliar with. More trees had fallen in the snow, making this man's tracks broader than the ones Notail used to hunt. The human odor persisted even after washing. Still, he was invisible to man, a half-seen shadow to them, a rustling, a spark of crimson, a figure darting between shadows.

Hungry, he went out in search of food. Foraging was his hobby. He told his father, "Forgive me, Father; I'm too hungry to care." As well as being too lonely. Some moldy meat and a chunk of rock-hard, stale man food that disintegrated into dust were among the items he discovered. He was unsatisfied with either the meat or the man's food. He was constantly reminded that each mouthful was uniquely his. No one else was there to enjoy it any longer.

He attempted to enter an open manden but was met with a hiss from the resident cat. The man called at the cat and Notail fled. Not even a cat could get him worked up today.

His nose led him along shadow tracks in search of food, but he found nothing. These manmade paths were much too neat and silent. Once he spotted a rat but it disappeared before he even made a move. That which casts a shadow. Alone. just like him.

When the main tracks petered out into the open country, he followed a line of an intertwined mattress constructed of gleaming rhinestone, whose high silver edge he knew could not be bitten through or vaulted. For a considerable number of paw falls, they headed westward. Always looking to the west. Towards the Manless Land.

Even though he could still smell humans, he could also detect forest and wildlife aromas.

As he stopped to listen for where a squirrel was scurrying he heard something snarling and, looking towards the shimmering mantras, he saw the shadow.

He had a firm grasp of the nature of the object. The aroma was really powerful. However, all he could make out was a blur of darkness and a pair of crimson, unmoving eyes.

It was a black dog.

Behind a thicket of mangroves, the Black Dog kept an eye on him. There was a recoil from Notail.
"Stay…fox," whispered the Black Dog, his voice as thick as a man's. The aroma of men filled the air.

In contrast to the shadow Notail aspired to be, the Black Dog was one. It's darker than the darkest black.

The Black Dog came closer to the shimmering mattress that separated them. Still, he was hidden by the darkness.

To wit: "What do you want?" As he continued to shrink back, Notail inquired.

With a deep sigh, the Black Dog finally spoke.

"What…man…want," the Black Dog said. "All…fox…end."

"End me?" said Notail. How dare you kill me?" I only seek true food and never harm man's young.

"You…run…now."

The black dog's mouth was streaming with saliva, and Notail could see it. Notail observed colossal canine teeth as the dog opened its jaws. Sharp and stained with blood.

"I...know...you...fox...no...tail" The shadowed canine drew nearer. The creature's nose was all rippling up.

"I...know...your...scent." Then it paused, and a grin crossed its face.

“I...know...your...den”

Notail halted his retreat. He wanted to leap the high edge and tear the huge dog apart. It did not bother him if the Black Dog ate him alive. That was irrelevant.

'My den,' Notail proudly proclaimed.

The Black Dog grinned and licked his teeth.

It referred to "your den." “Your mate your cubs. Go fox I hunt you.”

The notail snarled. The crest was excessively high. There was one more roar, and then he turned and was gone. Immediately, he took out in a westerly direction. Always looking to the west.

Chapter 7: A River, a Rowan Tree, and an Owl Without Answers

There was a river on the outskirts of the stone forest, and at the river's widest point, two-man tracks with arched bridges spanned the water. Both were used by both man carriers and individual soldiers. The sun had just risen, and there were very few people about. In addition to being thirsty, Notail's jogging had worn her out. To get water, he proceeded over the second man's track and down to the river.

While he was splashing about in the pool, he caught a glimpse of his reflection. Inverted and reflected. He reflected on his cubs and how in them he saw a reflection of himself. There was a time when it was a good thing, a bundle of promise. To think that they were holding a picture of him in their minds made his stomach turn. He averted his gaze from the ocean.

When Notail turned to see who was calling, he saw an owl sitting in a nearby rowan tree.

West, according to Notail.

“Why?”
Notail was unsure.

His ultimate response was, "To locate the Pale Fox in the Manless Land." He resumed his riverside drinking. The owl was the worst bird because it never stopped probing for knowledge.

Asking, "Do you know the path to this Manless Land?" requested the owl.

To which Notail just shrugged.

To the west, he proclaimed.

The owl then responded, "I see." In contrast, you should be aware that the west is empty except for the sleeping sun. My flight there was smooth and uneventful. To have faith in a Manless Land is ridiculous.

After finishing his drink, Notail ambled over to a nearby rowan tree. At the owl in the sky, he gazed. It has tiny, lengthy ears. That thing seemed to get a kick out of asking lots of questions.

The owl's head jerked rapidly in both directions.

“Is there decent hunting in the west?” asked Notail.

The owl's head bobbed once more.

"Why on earth would I tell you that?" He hooted once and took off into the night sky, expanding his wings.

As the owl flew away from the river, Notail watched it pass above the trees. A wordless peel of Manson and a spike of stone hacked from a group of maidens floated through the woods. The owl flew towards the spike, to roost inside it. Sunrise has arrived. Notail ran down the riverbed away from the sounds of people. West. West is always the direction we go.

Chapter 8: The Fieldsman

In the distance, Notail could make out the horizon. The sun rose in the east, bathing the earth in its reawakening light. All the life he had lived in that world. He had a different perspective on it now. The path through the stone forest had already been carved out. The whole lot. Existence on Earth is somewhat illuminated by fresh dawn light. The light emanated. The morning was as bright and clean as a summer day, thanks to the lights inside the maidens, the sun's reflection on rhinestones, and the pristine whiteness that coated everything.

This was once his stone forest, stretching from north to south, but he recognized almost none of it. The distance was enormous. It was as though he were gazing into a foreign land. Never really knew before. Distance separated them. Luminous and stony. His lair was buried amid all that brightness and stone. As for precisely where he had no idea. Take a deep intake of the cold air, he did, and then he turned away.

It was in the west that he found the world he had never before experienced. That odd and dark planet was still sleeping. There was no stone forest weighing down the landscape. A landscape of gently undulating hills and meadows, with snow ensnared around every turn. A stone forest this wasn't. In the stone forest, everything had a beginning and an end. The sheer size of it did not frighten him. Here and there he saw grey clumps of maidens, illuminated only by the artificial light of humans. The western globe seemed endless. His paws were ready to take him home, to the safety and security of the stone forest. However, he did not change his direction to avoid the west. He had to keep moving, he told himself, until the human world disappeared and only the foxes' homeland remained, the one they had abandoned so long ago but were doomed to forget. Where they have no men is in the west.

Walking over the icy meadows, he made his way. Sheep appeared here and there, scattered everywhere, nearly invisible in the snow until their dark heads sprung up to meet his. One stood, its black head turned toward Notail as he came closer. In his mind, he was a sheep hunter, but as he considered the possibility, more and more sheep rose to their feet to observe him. He left the sheep behind and continued westward towards the hills. West is always the direction we go.

The maidens of this stone forest are not all there is to the earth, his father had informed him.

Notail never really trusted his dad. When he was a cub, their stone forest seemed to go on forever. Right up to this point. Now, as he looked out across

unfamiliar territory, he understood that it was the planet itself that was infinite.
Padding down the hill, he continued forth, avoiding more encounters with the black-headed sheep. Every once in a while, he would pause to listen for something—a lone animal hunting, the sound of human footsteps, etc. There was silence save for the gentle breeze and the sound of birds in the distance. Thankfully, there was no noise from a man-carrying vehicle. Don't slam the door shut. There will be no rough-and-tumble macho talk.

Also missing were the familiar aromas associated with human habitation. There were authentic aromas all around this country. the sheep's wet wool. The feces of. The fresh aroma of their young. The shady muck and hidden grass. The lichen and moss. Ancient odors mingled with the peaty air. Heavy with bracken fern. Even the frigid air felt different, cleaner. He took a deep lungful and absorbed it. It was cold and odd. He inhaled it in again. That was a pleasant surprise.

He sat down on a stone edge that was just a few inches high. None of his paws felt tender. Their eyes met his. They had become tough and calloused from cushioning man tracks for so long. They'd never before walked on such solid ground. He examined the snow still stuck on his paw. Excellent snowfall. Purified snow. His body was pressed up against the stones as he attempted to sleep, a sign of how exhausted he felt. Not even close to sleep. The more I sleep, the more likely it is that I will dream, and if I do, it will only be of them, he reasoned to himself. Instead, he shut his eyes and listened to the quiet of the world.

The foxes' chattering woke him up. He believed for a second that the vixen whose voice he had heard had come to locate him and be his mate. His pulse was pounding, but when he peered over the edge he saw just four foxes and no cubs.

Stone forest foxes, he realized. They seemed to be as bewildered by the vastness and unfamiliarity of the outdoors as he was.

When they saw him, they stopped.

The vixen greeted him with a kind "hello."

When compared to his partner, she couldn't have been more different. White spots appeared in her fur, indicating that she was quite a bit older. They were different colors; her left eye was blue and her right eye was green. She gave him a kind grin, but he couldn't muster a return smile.

A man strolled in front of her, padding. He was burly and rough around the edges.

The man addressed her directly, "Are you alone?" He focused his attention on the remaining portion of Notail's tail.
Notail responded affirmatively. He took a peek at the two younger people. They may have easily been the vixen and male's grown cubs.

Have you been through the stone forest?" the vixen enquired.

No tailing nod. Rather than engaging them, he ignored them. The fox cub stared after him till he returned home.

Not to worry, she reassured me. As far as I can see, no canines are trailing after us.

He realized, to his dismay, that "one" was following him. His silence was deliberate. They were young, and he glanced at one of them; he knew they were afraid.

"There are a lot of dogs in the stone forest these days," the guy replied. His tone of the speech was deep and rough. They're on the prowl. Some birds have reported the death of a human cub. My family and I are relocating to the south. Southern rumors include the presence of lakes and forests. Greetings, hunters!

Yes, that's what you said, Notail.

Even the man looked back for a second. He doesn't know who or what is following me, or what I may bring with me, thought Notail.

The vixen said, "Where are you going?"

Notail just started talking like that. They arrived confidently. In the strongest possible terms.

He said, "I'm heading west." I'm on the hunt for the Pale Fox.

The baby foxes glanced at their dad. A masculine voice chuckled. The sly fox remained silent.

The man muttered to Notail, "You're an idiot," and continued walking past him. Instead of smelling for the odor of a myth, you should discover a location to hunt and a place to dwell.

In contrast to her mate's sharp comments, the vixen's tone was soothing as she invited us to join them. Her partner gave her an angry look.

As he did so, Notail shook his head.

He was unable to come along. It was preferable to be alone, if only for a little while. His only option was to be completely alone. Foxes might be pursued in the same manner as he was without the use of paws. He cast his gaze on the fox cubs. There are two of them, and their tails are just gorgeous. It used to be that they had a hideout of some kind. The two of them would have been great friends on the playground. To have fun, they would have joined their tough dad in playing. Of course not; he had to go westward exploration all on his own. Taking the southern route was not his option but rather theirs. He decided to go in a westerly direction. West is always the direction we go.

The younger ones followed their father but the vixen remained. Her expression was one of awe as she observed him.

Inquiringly, "Are you genuinely trying to locate him?" she probed.

Even when the male yelled at her to follow, she remained in place.

Notail responded affirmatively to her inquiry. I'm hitting the road for the western hemisphere. The Manless Land is where I intend to go.

With a grin on her face, she continued. Never before has he seen eyes like them on a fox.

You will, she assured me.

Once again, the male barked, and this time the vixen ran after her partner. After the four foxes had disappeared into the distance, Notail remained at the edge of the stone slab. They made their way southward slowly. Notail pondered whether or if the man was correct and whether or not there was decent hunting and woods in that direction. However, he was skeptical. No, he told himself, it was not the west; it was merely man's world.

Chapter 9: Once Upon a Time, There Was a Young Dog Tied to a Tree

The young puppy was chained to a tree in the middle of a white field with thick twists of man grass. The field was blanketed with snow, and the puppy looked miserable.

Like this dog, Notail has seen others in the stone forest. Their lords, who were constantly furious and shirtless, kept them at the end of rhinestone chains. Notail knew that canines like these existed since he'd read about foxes being pursued by them. Watching the hunt while sipping on fetid water and puffing on fire twigs was a typical pastime for early humans.

Notail hid on the snow-covered grass and kept an eye on the puppy.

It had lost hope. The dried blood was just next to where the man's grass had been wrapped around its neck. Intensely bitter odors permeated the atmosphere. There were several ancient wounds on the young dog's snout. Blood clots crusted on its closed eyelids. The young dog's chest was visible to Notail as it progressively expanded and contracted. Loser but still breathing.

Notail approached, but even when the puppy's eyes opened he did not rise to his feet.

“Who tied you here?” Notail asked.

The little dog closed his eyes again and groaned. He was extremely young.

“I don’t know,” he responded, his voice quiet and fresh. “I was asleep and I awakened here. I don’t feel well. There is too much of this place.”

Notail stepped closer. He remained low, ready to flee. He knew not to trust dogs, especially young ones.

“Is your master near?” Notail asked. The aroma of a male was faint.

“I don’t know,” responded the young dog. The answer is probably not, "I don't believe I have one anymore."

Notail scanned the blank area around him. Only the snow and a lone bird were there as observers. That pup knew what he was talking about; the area beyond the stone forest was very enormous. He cast his gaze to the west and pondered how much further it would be before he reached the Manless Land. His journey might take several years. Unlike the stone forest, this

realm had no walls. There was no end to this universe of field and hill and forest and stream.
Notail approached the pup to take a smell of the man's grass.

Attempting to eat some man grass, he got a little too much. The little dog remained still during Notail's man grass-chewing session, his eyes shut tightly as if he were sleeping. Notail prodded the puppy when he saw that he had finally broken through the man's grass.

Notail said, "Get up and go on your way."

Complete lucidity returned to the puppy's eyes. He surveyed the mangled man's grass and then turned to study Notail.

The puppy responded, "You shattered it for me." The man got to his feet. His coat was a dingy, filthy yellow, and it was matted with thick, bloody tufts.

Notail said, "I did." "What's your name, dog?"

The young dog shook his head.

I don't think so," he remarked. "There are moments when I suspect I may have had one, but I can never recall it," he said.

Notail said, "Every animal deserves a name." Even a man's best friend."

Notail withdrew his body.

The puppy followed him and questioned, "Where are you going?"

I'm heading west to discover the Pale Fox and the Manless Land," Notail said. Not in my head, please.

Chapter 10: Discussions with a Pup

It took the pup two days to catch up to Notail. Notail awaited the arrival of the pup the next day at the base of a rhinestone man tree buzzing with songbirds. As he approached, Notail observed him cautiously. As a result, he was frail and underweight. The fox shook his head. If I don't assist him, he'll die, he told himself. It seemed like everything in Notail's life came to an end.

With that, Notail commanded, "Rest," and the puppy curled up and went to sleep.

Notail clarified, "I said relax, not sleep." To keep heading westward is imperative.

The puppy blinked his eyes wide and looked up at Notail.

We, he proclaimed. If so, "May I tag along?"

Notail padded over to the side and inspected the mantra above him. He had the impression that man likes to build things very tall. The clouds were moving over the sky, and he noticed it. He pondered whether or not that was what mantras were designed to catch.

Did they go out to track down clouds themselves? Insight into human behavior eluded him.
At long last, he responded positively. I invite you to accompany me. Have some downtime, since we'll be leaving soon.

Notail did not disturb the young puppy from his profound slumber. Instead, he saw clouds roll in and snow begin to fall from the sky. He laid back and allowed the snow to cover his whole body, including his nose, ears, and short tail. He awakened the puppy up when the clouds broke and he noticed that the sun was at its peak.

A native of the stone forest could ask, "Are you from around here?" When did they leave the rhinestone man tree, Notail inquired.

The pup pondered the topic for a time.

In the long end, he said, "I don't know." When I think back to the place I slept, I see a hard, chilly floor. Never warm, always frigid. Sometimes a guy would bring me water. From high up in its maiden, a man-cub would keep an eye on me.

Have you ever gone on a hunting trip?" Asked Notail.

Once, a rat got into the room where I slept, the pup remarked. However, "I didn't want to harm him."

What do you eat then?" Asked Notail.
The little dog mostly ate human food, he claimed. I don't have much success.

Notail took the pup hunting and fed him everything he caught. Not that much ever came of it. For Notail, this was all still very foreign and unfamiliar territory. There were no concealed places for him to sneak inside.

The young puppy looked up into the clear sky on a day when the sun was shining and the snow had stopped falling.

The puppy questioned, "What is that?" Although there were other questions he enjoyed, this one was his favorite. Is it safe for consumption? What if it eats me? Whence comes the weeping of the heavens? Can I reach the sun with one giant leap? What's with the mushy soil? The question of where the world ends. Do you think I couldn't share your foxes? A dog would understand why you're not one, right?

As the cloud echoes died down, a man bird made its way gently through them.

Notail said to the young dog, "Man wants to be more than a man." Many birds, mancarriers, and man-fish are all products of their factory. They want to claim the heavens above as part of their territory as well.

The pup saw the man bird become a distant dot in the western sky before it finally disappeared. It's always westward.

But not the Manless Land," the pup emphasized.

Notail said, "No." "We're not there yet."

The puppy's eyes never left the spot where the man bird had been.

Notail replied, "We need to keep going," but the little dog would not budge.

It's not "I'm not a guy anymore, am I?" inquiringly the pup canine.

"Notail" moaned.

Perhaps not, he said. The two of us should keep pushing forward, however.

Despite repeated encouragement, the puppy did not make any attempt to follow.

The puppy then said, "I'm with you now." With you, I know I'm secure.

Notail was at a loss for words. He gave a dismissive shake of the head and shuffled off. The pup eventually decided to tag along.

Chapter 11: The Big Hunt

Over time, they arrived at a desolate mansion. They saw a man carrier come to life and whisk a lady and her man cubs away. The second guy transporter did not wake up.

A cow stood with her hooves in the snow, confined by a short stone wall. There were a lot of people on the grass within that perimeter. There were fewer maidens here than in the Stoneforest, and the area was more natural.

Bone inquired, "What is the cow for?"

Perhaps, mused Notail, they were unable to locate a suitable dog.

There was no reaction from the cow.

The pup questioned whether or not it was allowed to hunt.

Not that, Notail scowled at the cow. It's on a scale that makes ending it impossible. We'll come up with a solution.

In this case, Bone was wagging his tail enthusiastically.

What do you mean, "And I can hunt that?" "Bone," the man said.

A nod was given by Notail.

Recall that "if we locate anything, you need to remain low, be silent, and pounce immediately," he warned.

The puppy gave a little nod.

They went all the way around the manden but it was securely locked. Inside the fridge, Notail saw a chicken that had been transformed by fire. He vowed he would never eat another chicken.

Once Notail pointed, Bone looked in the same direction. The man carrier was parked next to a sleeping wild bunny.

Getting ready, Notail asked.

That's what the pup figured, at least.

Notail emphasized, "Remember, feel no remorse." As a dog, you have dietary requirements. Act rapidly, strike hard, and wrap things up fast. It's best if it doesn't find out what's going on.

A young dog advanced. His snout was wagging like crazy. He seemed to be about to make a lunge with his hind legs, which were twitching.

Nothing happened to the bunny. Like it had found its permanent home, it remained parked next to the man carrier.

After hearing "now" from Notail, the pup bolted. The rabbit then started to make a move. It quickly darted beneath the man-carrier. The puppy continued to yap crazily and run beside Notail, completely oblivious to his warnings. He squeezed through the little opening, and suddenly they were both on their way again. While the young dog was awkward and slower than the rabbit, both were quick on their feet. All in the route of the little puppy were objects that were smashed. We tossed out some flower holes, and scrapemakers, and changed trees, leafenders, and stone.

There was no attempt at avoidance on the part of the puppy. Notail was astounded by the racket he created. Notail realized that the key to a successful hunt was silence. It was crucial for a hunter to establish his own space of stillness, to move without contributing to the clamor of the stoneforest. Unfortunately, the young dog contributed little except noise and confusion to the pursuit. Everything was in such disarray.

Both the rabbit and the puppy withdrew from view behind the manden. There was a lot of banging and clattering that nobody could hear. Finally, he caught sight of the rabbit once again. Its eyes were fixed on him. Perhaps it even flashed a grin. In its mind, the puppy had no chance of catching it. An angry rumble came from Notail. As the puppy reappeared behind him panting, he told himself, "Enough." Hunting is a talent to be acquired, and the puppy will have plenty of other opportunities to do so in the future. When Notail saw the pursuit, he gave chase, too. A swift death for the rabbit and a lesson for the pup would be the result. You need to speed up. Try to quicken your thoughts. Rapid action is required.

But by the time Notail had started running, the rabbit was already gone. The only other sounds were those of the cow observing and panting in the snow, and the young dog's head cocking in every direction as it searched for the rabbit.

They moved forward in a padded fashion to the spot where the rabbit had been. A break or void was present. It was gloomy there. The bunny had vanished.

The puppy sniffed the opening.

With an effort, he questioned, "Can I fit?" and he pushed himself into the opening. Just his head squeaked in there.
“Stop,” snapped Notail and The little dog froze. There's no need to even trying. Nothing remains.

The puppy said, "I'm sorry." His expression radiated despondency. With that defeated expression, Notail felt helpless to reprimand him.

Notail reasoned, "He'll die eventually, so I may as well attempt to make him a hunter." There is no greater training than watching me hunt, he reminded himself, so he should just let him watch.

There will be more to discover, Notail promised. You're going to grow up to be a real hunter.

The little dog's face quickly lost its look of dismay and he broke out into a broad grin.

The puppy answered with a wagging tail, "I will." Eventually, I shall become just as skilled a hunter as you are.

There was no response from Notail. There was a time when he would have laughed at any creature that spoke such a thing, but not now. No longer did it bother him. The pup would benefit from maturing into a skilled hunter. Perhaps, he reflected, I was never a genuine hunter. He took a tour of the grey sludgy grass that surrounded the manden. The cow had given up on digging for food in the snow and was now staring at them. The puppy had smashed every fragile object he could find.

There was an unhappy rumble in Notail's gut. And he needed to eat badly. It would have been nice to have eaten a rabbit.

Saying, "Come on, there is nothing here but manthings," he urged us to leave.

He abandoned the puppy to stare into the abyss. Cattle yawned.

Chapter 12: An Idyll in the Cavern of Recollections

Together, they climbed steep slopes and entered the thick forest beyond. West. Always west.

I'm hungry, the pup said for the umpteenth time.

Notail lifted its nose to the air and smelled. The mild aroma of rabbit was present. In an exasperated manner, he yawned. That's why he was trying to go to bed so early. He hoped to sleep forever and never wake up. On the other hand, his hunger growled at him, and the young dog's stomach growled back.

Notail said, "Stay close to me." Make no noise. Can you pull it off?

The puppy gave a little nod.

You couldn't even compare it to the stone forest in the woods. There was an animal odor in the air. Small animals like mice, squirrels, rabbits, and even birds were all detectable to Notail's keen sense of smell. Imagine a world in which real aromas predominated rather than the artificial ones often associated with men.

Young dogs' tail wags when they discover bunnies. Notail said, "Remember, remain quiet."

The search was also unique this time. The world was not so quiet in the stone forest. This forest was completely silent. There was complete silence among the bunnies. No sound of the wind could be heard. The puppy didn't make any noise at all. There was complete silence from Notail. They hid under the low, dark, and safe of a fallen tree. The rabbits were digging through the snow to get to the fresh grass below. A few of them seemed to be dozing off. Young rabbits were visible, but they were spread out throughout the expanse of grass. He'd probably go for the elderly rabbit closest to them.

So he waited for the aging rabbit to go away. Is to contemplate taking a nap. You'd think he'd be content and secure if he were full of grass. Suddenly, Notail sprang at him. Other rabbits ran away, but Notail quickly pounced on the elderly rabbit before it could get away. Notail gave the elderly rabbit a sharp bite to the neck and the rabbit stopped crying.

They split the rabbit in two.

The puppy said, "It tastes better than man food."

The meat was quite rough. This is some very stale beef. At least it was meat, however.

The puppy commanded, "Look," and Notail turned to see across the clearing. Some of the bunnies looked on curiously.

This young puppy felt awful and stated so.

One of the elderly rabbit's legs was severed by Notail's tearing.

Do not ever feel remorse, Notail urged. If you allow yourself to feel remorse, it will be your last day. Just like all other creatures, you really must eat. As it is, this is the situation.

That's a good lesson, for now, Notail decided; he'll pick up many more, and fast.

As night fell, they snuggled up to one other in the hollow of an ancient tree.

Notail could hear the puppy shuffle about restlessly in his sleep.

The puppy called out, "Fox."

"Notail" moaned.
Notail explained, "My name is Notail, not the fox."

That's exactly what I was thinking of," the puppy replied. I was considering my moniker if you will. But

I don't know any names, so I'm left speculating what they may be. That's not the case at all.

A single eye sprung out on Notail. Within the pitch-black wood, he could make out how little

There was a young dog. His bare-bones poked through his fur.

Notail, eyes closed, murmured, "You should be named Bone."

The puppy expressed approval. "I like the moniker Bone. What do you think of me if I tell you my name is Bone?

'Yes,' agreed Notail. We'll see you in the morning, Bone.

There was a brief moment of calm before he heard the frantic shuffling resume.

The puppy called out, "Fox." Sorry, I meant Notail.

Notail let out another sigh.
What is it now?" he finally inquired.

I had another question. I was wondering whether your tail is as well. When Bone was curious, he enquired.

There was a grin on Notail's face.

Notail informed him, "I exchanged it for a shank of fire changed pig."

Bone let out a sharp intake of breath, which he heard.

While they slept, he overheard the puppy repeating, "Bone," to himself. It was an excellent choice, and the little canine seemed to be very happy with his new moniker.

The time for sleep has come. Notail gave in to the feeling and let it overtake him.

Dreams about his family, including his mate and pups, occupied his sleep. Wildflowers and the lake appeared in his dreams. When he first laid eyes on her. She, too, remained nameless.

'I've never needed one,' she said to him.

Notail instructed the fox, "Every fox needs a name."

She turned her gaze to the weeds. A butterfly floated gracefully over the blossoms, dancing. The bees drank the nectar. A flock of ducks quacked on the water. A white wildflower petal was carried away by the wind.

After being hoisted for a split second, it landed in front of them, not far from their paws.
She turned her gaze to the blossoms.

Wildflower is my favorite," she said.

As for him, he enjoyed it as well. That worked for her. I mean, she went crazy.

The term, "Wildflower," he said gently. In a kind gesture, he nuzzled her.

Something changed in his dream. He kept visualizing the day and night his cubs were born. On the first night, he was wide awake the entire time. While his mate and pups slept, Notail continued repeating the names his mate had given them.

In a glimpse, he caught sight of his partner.

He called her a "wildflower," and she brightened up.

She nuzzled his neck and murmured, "If you locate the Pale Fox." I may or may not show up.

He finally responded, "You are gone."

She gave him another nuzzle.
I do know, she admitted.

There was another change in the dream. He did not want it to. He wished he could remain in his dream and continue sleeping indefinitely. However, the dream turned against him. A shadow appeared in his dreams. When it got too close, it entered their cave. The cubs started calling out for dad. He cried out his partner's name, but it sounded mournful. Not a pushover. That's ugly. It's over now. Something stopped him from approaching them, digging its paw into his back and forcing him to the ground.

He yelled, "Let go of me!" but was still unable to release himself.

The puppy was snarling at the darkness as he woke up. Something was stirring among the woods just beyond the oak's hollow.

Chapter 13: To Put a Smile on a Panting Dog's Face

"I smell a dog," Bone said.

Notail squinted into the shadows. The only sounds were those of the night and the odd rustling. However, the same odor followed him inside his cave. Notail realized it had been here before. Not even close to being located. It was at Bone that he turned for guidance. Notail mused, "He smells Bone, but my scent is lessened." It's not quite there yet, but it's near.

The aroma pierced the air like a dagger. Perhaps it was not too far away.

Notail emphasized the urgent urgency to flee the scene. To the westward, we must flee!

I can't tell you the direction west," Bone said.

Although Notail saw nothing as he turned around, he was aware of its presence. A deeper, second blackness nested inside the night's first blackness.

They continued to run.
With Notail at the helm, they emerged from the forest and into a claustrophobic assemblage of maidens. As

they sprinted, he could hear each paw hitting the ground. They walked by manden after manden, each one illuminating with a brief flash of light. A man's voice could be heard yelling. Then a woman's scream of terror echoed across the air. Notail realized, "She's seen it," so he accelerated his pace. They used man tracks as a climbing surface, shot down other people using man tracks, and kept going.

A voice called out "Dark, dark, dark," as four crows circled over them.

'Run fox,' they yelled. We advise immediate action: "Run, run, run."

He cast an eye in the other direction. The road they had come was brilliant with the false light of mandates now and in the crevices between those lights, he spotted a shadow moving. He was confident of it. In the pitch dark of night, there is a deeper black. It never came into the light. The thing remained hidden in the shadows.

Keep on going, Notail yelled back at Bone.

The little dog was weary but Notail would not stop.

Notail warned, "It is coming."
His ears picked up Bone's frantic breathing.

They hurriedly slid down the slippery main track and hopped over the stone edge into the tall grass below. The grass was sharp with ice. The grass wasn't as tall near the far end of the field, and that's where Notail saw them. A pack of four foxes. One, a man, stood ahead of the others ready to battle.

He peered up into the night sky, but couldn't tell west from the south. That's why I came down here, he told himself.

Notail looked back briefly. It is coming, he thought.

He screamed, "Run!" and continued running. "Run, he's coming!"

The male eyed the maidens, and with bark, the four foxes bolted from Notail and Bone and disappeared into the forest.

Notail could hear Bone behind him wheezing and panting for air. Suddenly, there was a massacre of crows in the sky. Their cry was far but he heard it enough. The time to act is now.

“Keep running,” said Notail so on they ran.

They bounded over a squat stone edge and into thick shrubs. Soon they were rushing by more maidens. Sad, alone people. Mandeans hanging to the edge of

the wild. Notail saw a lady sprinkling man food over the frozen grass. The lady was being observed by a cat.
He kept turning around to take another look. Despite Bone's significant distance behind him, the pup kept on running. Within a short while, nothing but darkness surrounded them. No pursuing shadow. There was no scream to break the universe. It's time to roar now. Those aren't any falling claws.

Notail could feel his heart breaking, his lungs stuttering. He thought about Bone. I have abandoned him, he murmured to himself and he stopped running.

They were at the line of maidens' end and a moor waited for them just beyond a desolate man track.

"Why have we stopped?" muttered Bone, gasping. I don't feel exhausted just yet.

The pup was at a loss for words.

The main track was poorly lighted, and Notail cast his eyes along it. The noise of a man-carrier woke me up, but otherwise, there was nothing.

"We are safe," replied Notail. Bone cracked a grin. A little white lie to make a panting dog happy is better than no lie at all. The truth was something different.

The reality was something Notail could not conceal from himself. That dreaded Black Dog had tracked them down. And now it had their scent, it would keep hunting them. And it was only a matter of time before it found them again.

14th Chapter: Always Head South

You could see the moor rise and fall. They strolled well into the evening, beyond the time when the sun would have been asleep. The snow had become chilly and damp on their paws. Notail would sometimes look about, but he always came up empty. Eventually, they were both weary. Notail drew to a halt at a location where the land sloped down towards another grouping of grey stone maidens. He pondered why man lingered here on the moors when they had the stone forest to go to. Foxes should have the moors to themselves.

Suddenly, Bone perked up. He had a panoramic view of the moor before him.

When questioned, "What are they?" he pressed more for clarification.

There were stony formations up on the moor they had to climb. The snow was home to both towering and squat figures. They formed a circle around themselves, and other forms appeared inside the circle. Foxes seemed to Notail for a brief period, but they did not attempt to flee. He tried to reassure himself that it was only stone. Yet despite this, he

found himself drawn into the center of the group. There is a hint of fox in the air.
He instructed Bone to "stay here."

He made his way cautiously toward the boulders. Both ancient and mossy, they looked terrible. Humans are peculiar creatures, he thought to himself as he walked between them. They caught his eye at that very moment. A family of four foxes seemed to be fast asleep, with the offspring curled up next to mom and their paws practically touching. Very motionless, although not quite as still as a stone. There was just one of her eyes open. One of her eyes was a vibrant green. At the outside rim of the circle stood the father. The marks of the cats' claws were all over him. He was a veteran of several battles.

The reason they were there, though, was known to him. The reality of it struck him like a hammer. His aroma had mingled with the maidens in the meadow beyond them. He and Bone had gotten away, but it wasn't because of their speed or cunning. They lucked out. And the price had been paid by someone else.

He sincerely expressed regret and apologized.

His mind went to the father's fight. Protecting his loved ones. Suppressing a sob, he realized he would never be able to have it.
Returning to the Bone, he resumed his padded stroll.

He then urged the pup to "keep going" with him.
It seems to be following us even now. expressed Bone

It is," Notail confirmed. It would serve no use to lie once again. He realized now that he was unable to defend Bone. No risk of injury. The Black Dog is not where this comes from.

Notail turned around to face the ancient monuments he had passed on the moor. Only the two of them remained on the moor after everyone else had left. Notail reasoned that if he stayed with him, he would calm down and become inert.

Chapter 15: Farewell, and May the Manbird Reign Over Your Land

They continued their journey over the moor. They would stoop down to hide if they saw a human. A single guy was causing birds to crash to the ground by aiming an and sticking into the sky. Luckily, he was accompanied by his dog. Notail prayed that the dog wouldn't be able to sniff them. The dog perked up and followed their gaze across the moors, his ears perking up in the process.

This is what I mean," Notail remarked. "Even man has to hunt."

The guy was now observing them as well. He stood and observed them for quite some time before tapping his leg, at which point his dog returned, clutching a bird in his jaws. Before long, the guy was no longer there.

When Notail first saw the moor, he was not impressed. The only thing that could be seen around them was the moor. The Black Dog, he realized, was probably watching them. Following them about and trying to scare them off. I'm just waiting for the right moment to put an end to them. For a few seconds, he let his eyes shut and tried to see the Black Dog coming at him. Even if only in his head, he retaliated. Bravely. It was for the sake of his partner. As a sacrifice for his cubs. The battle was a tough one for him. A battle with the Black Dog ensued.

His eyes flickered open. Clouds were puffy and white in the distance to the west, and snow fell over the ground. He was aware that they were in for a tough battle if the Black Dog tracked them down.

He saw a man bird flying far above him, out of reach. To all appearances, it was doing nothing except moving slowly. Notail realized that nothing stays in one place for long.

Safety. He now understood that this was only fiction.

He cast his gaze on the pup. Even faster as he had transformed from the dog Notail had discovered tethered to the tree, Bone was undergoing a metamorphosis. In contrast to the thinness implied by the phrase. Not. His muzzle would never be the same, and he would always have the scars, yet his eyes were bright with life. Notail reflected, "He will never let go of that life now; I cannot lead him into danger."

Notail suggested that we stop at the mandates we had seen earlier. One possible solution is to locate a new master.

You are my master, right?" inquired Bone.
I am a fox," he said. That's because he's "no man."

But you called me, Bone countered. Can you think of anything else that men do?

Snapping, "I am not a man and you are not a fox," Notail made his point clear. A man will dispatch his dogs to kill a fox. Do you wish to meet the same fate as my family at the hands of the Black Dog? You can't understand what it's like to be the hunted. Right now, you should go out there and live. Leaving at this time will save us both from the Black Dog. Flesh and bone remained immobile.

What about the Pale Fox?" the puppy enquired. You claimed we would locate the Manless Land. I don't give a hoot about the Black Dog, but I would want to go along while you search for the Pale Fox.

Notail warned that "the Manless Land is a habitat for foxes and you are no fox." He knew he was being nasty, but he felt he had to say it. The man started running.

Notail reached a man track that across the moor and turned around to see that Bone was nowhere to be seen.

Chapter 16: The Meaning of a Broken Bird

In the west, the man track disappeared into the moor. Always looking to the west. It was a sleek grey trail, much like the many tracks in the stone forest, yet there were no man carriers in sight.

Notail discovered a dead, smashed bird near the man track. Notail had never seen this kind of bird before, but he nevertheless ate it. It had a stale, rabbit-like flavor, but he was too hungry to notice that the flesh was rough. The flavor wasn't bad, though. It was food.

The fact that he was standing on a man's track did not bother him. The regulations set out by his father were as far as the stone jungle. Dead and gone, just like his existence in that place. As he chewed, he pushed out of his mind the words his father had just spoken.

His dad had stated, "You couldn't ever fail me," and he believed it.

eons ago. That which came before and whatever comes after.

The bone was spat out by Notail.

"I have failed you," he murmured into the void. Don't bother me right now.

All communication ceased.

The stale meat was crushed and chewed before being sucked down.

Notail recoiled from the partially digested fowl. When the man carriers' lights came on, everything seemed bright and hazy for a second.

His whole body stiffened up. The man carries on the moor were unlike any he had seen before. A bright flash of light and the main carrier's terrifying roar stopped him in his tracks.

He thought back on the comrades who had been flung to the stone banks, their corpses in pieces. Man has chosen to ignore it. He was curious about the experience. He felt the man-weight carriers press down on him. There was nothing left of him; his body was shattered and lifeless.

The moor was devoid of any stone walls. Just like the bird he had just eaten, he would be left for dead on the man track. Maybe another animal would come along and eat him. Who knows, maybe that was for the best. The natural order of things

The troop transport came racing up quickly. The spotlights trapped him and temporarily blinded him. His paw was raised. He had some mobility. He could approach the manned transport and allow himself to be killed. Allow it to suffocate him into oblivion. It wouldn't be hard at all.

Notail hoped that the manned transport would keep arriving.

There was a manned cart approaching him. The thing made a tremendous noise.

No. No, not just now.

A moment later, he was already on the go. To avoid the glare, he sprang off the man track. The man kept going and going.

He landed on the icy grass. He saw the man carriers rapid departure, which was accompanied by a blast of wind and a cloud of dust.

The tail flopped down. Panting. Breathing. Alive.

He shut his eyes, and his father's voice echoed in his head.

Bone. He shook his head, but it didn't make what he'd done any less real. I shouldn't have left him, he told himself, since he was all he had.

No tail up. Yes, he thought to himself as the main carrier's lights disappeared into the night on the moor, he is my family now, I am all he has. He took a deep breath of the fresh air and took off at that. Going in reverse of his first route. Go back over the moor. It's time to go back to the bone.

Chapter 17: When Stars Go Down is

Notail turned around and stared at the stars as he raced back over the moors. Very few stars had been visible to him in the stone jungle. Throughout history, there has never been any true illumination other than that which was created by humans. Overhead, in the blackness, the world continued forever. Now that he had arrived, he understood his proper role. In other words, he was no longer a lone fox bewildered in the stone age. To put it another way, he had company. It wasn't only the stars up there, there were stars everywhere. A huge nothingness is devoid of terror. A lot of them. He had never considered that number was even possible.

A star had fallen, he realized, a pinpoint of fire hurtling toward Earth with incredible velocity. A tail was even present on this creature.

The rain was pouring westward.

He paused to take a deep breath of air. The smell of Bone was very weak, and he now knew it was neither up ahead nor to the east. Despite its seeming distance, it originated in the west. Notail smiled to himself as he realized he was heading west.

Notail continued running in the direction of the vanishing star, following the smell that had led him there. More stars were falling as he rushed. Flares of intense light cut through the darkness. He was perplexed as to their motivations. No matter what the stars were, they were probably not supposed to fall from the sky. It was their mission to shine, just as it had been their mission to hunt in the stone forest. To protect his pups and wife. Even stars have to go on, he realized.

There was no stopping Notail as he headed westward. He sped off in a determined, nonstop dash.

He paid little attention to the length of time he had been running or the fact that he was exhausted. The aroma of Bone became more pungent with each thump of his paw. At long last, he reached a forest.

He took a whiff of the forest. This was the spot where Notail detected the aroma the strongest, yet he stopped to take it all in. He felt trapped in the forest's gloom and didn't enjoy it. For a split second, he wondered what was beyond the forest. Something that casts a shadow. A more ominous kind of nighttime. There was an audible snarl from him. Now was not the time to let his concerns stop him. He knew Bone was in there somewhere; if he wasn't, he wouldn't be able to locate him.

His plea into the forest, "Bone," was met with silence. His paw was rubbing on his neck as he did this. More stars above him broke out of the darkness and rushed down toward Earth. He loped towards the forest, and the night sky quickly became obscured by treetops.

He made his way down through the woods slowly, following the little dog's smell. The tree line was rather short. When he emerged through the other side, he saw a large pit in the stone that had been excavated by human hands, but there was no Bone there. Notail cautiously approached the precipice and peeked over. There was a significant vertical drop to a rocky landscape below.

Notail took a good look at the weird location he had found himself in while trying to find Bone. The stars were out again in the sky above him, but the depression below him was pitch black.

The forest was beginning to close in on him from behind. This cornered him and he couldn't get out. Covering up in the dark. A possible case of covering one's eyes. The odd depression was there in front of him. Somewhere empty and uninteresting. The stone, the muck, the grass, everything had been removed by man, and now there was nothing but quiet and vast nothingness. It wasn't a great spot, but the puppy dog's smell was close by. It's an insurmountable deficit, and now would be a terrible time to lose. Way too close to losing now.

Behind him, the leaves on the trees began to stir.

The trees shifted. Expectedly, something would happen.

Then he realized what it was. Its form. The darkness.

And a low snarl accompanied it. Despite the situation, he showed no signs of fear. Fear had left him, and he felt only a strong urge to guard Bone as he would have his cubs. For Bone, he was prepared to risk everything.

What he needed was for the Black Dog to show up.

Notail reflected, "It has found me," as he prepared to face the Black Dog.

Chapter 18: Viewing Fear

Notail said to the woods, "I am prepared."

A low growl was his response.

As though scraping out the words, "ready to take my rats," a voice muttered. I've seen your tricks before, fox.

It emerged from the thicket of trees, but it wasn't a dog. It sat lower to the ground and had a stockier build. The Black Dog couldn't have been fatter. Similar in age to the old. Its fur was becoming grey where it had formerly been white against black, and its eyes were wet.

Notail was familiar with badgers. They would sometimes go to the stone forests fringes, where the real forest met the world of humans. As a rule, he would not interact with them.

The badger studied Notail intently.

It proclaimed, "A fox and a dog close by the smell of it." Easily put together. Still, Hardclaw's confronted more and sent them to the hollow. NO WAY are you getting my rats.

Notail sighs a sigh of relief. With a quick look around, he attempted to find Bone. The badger was correct. The pup wasn't far away.

The badger advanced on us. In addition to being large, it was also cumbersome and sluggish. A monster capable of giving Notail the scrap it craved.

Notail firmly said, "I have not come for your rats." "I was only trying to find my pal."

Shaking his striped head, Hardclaw said nothing.

"Hardclaw knows your game," the badger said. You foxes are usually lurking about Hardclaw's property, looking for a tasty morsel of a rat. On the other hand, this is my territory. Crap, that's a shame. That's not your territory, you fox.

The badger's muzzle puffed out. Its brown fangs were visible to Notail. Tactical and armed to the teeth.

Saying, "I simply want to go on my way," Notail expressed his desire to go. The rats are yours to keep.

He attempted to retreat, but the badger followed him.

There's no else for you to go, fox, the badger said. That which you are planning, I am aware of. I know if I send you on your way, you'll brag to your other foxes about my rats. If Hardclaw releases you, he won't have any rats left. And Hardclaw doesn't like to go hungry.

Notail started to walk again, but the badger snarled at him before he could get more than a pawfall away.

The fox was told, "No, the hollow is where you belong." Even if they don't talk much, you'll have enough foxes to keep you company down there.

As he said this, Hardclaw let out a chuckle. There was a croaky chuckle. There was a stifled, scraping chuckle.

The hollow caught Notail's eye, and he cast a backward look. He was curious as to the depth of it.

Again, Notail stated, "I simply want to continue on my way," but he knew it would be difficult after meeting the badger's moist eyes. A brawl is certain here. It was a battle, but not the one Notail was expecting. Eventually, he let out a heavy sigh.

The badger emphasized that no foxes nor dogs should bother with Hardclaw's rats. As the saying goes, "Hardclaw battled for his territory, and he will never give it up. This is your last night, fox.

Badger made a growling noise and charged toward Notail. The animal sprang at the fox, its brown fangs as moist as its eyes.
The weight of Hardclaw sucked the wind from Notail. They landed on the ground below. Badger claws tore at Notail. The claws were sturdy but dull. Ratty claws. While the badger tried to bite Notail's throat, Notail retaliated with a series of sharp claw slashes. They repeated the motion again and over. The badger's foul breath was detectable to Notail. The smell of rats permeated the area.

Hardclaw snarled, "The hollow wants you, fox," and then he bit Notail's shoulder with his bare fangs.

Notail yelped in agony, and the two of them separated, each waiting for an opportunity to strike again.

When they were separated, Notail saw the physical effects of his attack on Hardclaw. Blood soaked his fur, and he was punctured all over. For his part, Notail only felt discomfort in his shoulder, and that hurt less and less as time went on. The badger seemed elderly, sluggish, injured, and exhausted. As he returned with his wild and almost crazed eyes, Notail almost felt bad for him.

Hardclaw slammed into Notail.

Over and over, they rolled. Fighting while rolling, claws scraping and shredding, Notail eventually kicked the badger away.

The hollow is calling you, fox; can you hear it? chuckled Hardclaw.

At that moment, Notail felt a wind brush over his tail stub and looked back to see that he had reached the very edge of the depression. If he took one more step, he'd join the foxes Hardclaw said. To top it all off, Notail was now really worried.

Hardclaw warned the fox, "You won't have any rats tonight." Instead of meat, you may eat the bones of your brothers.

Now that Notail was standing on the precipice, the badger's broad frame prevented him from escaping in either direction. This is not how it's supposed to end, Notail thought. no, not in this way.

With a last-ditch yelp, Harclaw dove at Notail.

You can't take my rats," he yelled at the fox.

He extended his forepaws. Sharp claws gleamed.

And along with him, something jumped.

Notail yelled, "Bone!" as the young dog smacked Hardclaw, sending the old badger flying to the side of the hollow's rim.

Hardclaw tried to get to his feet in a state of bewilderment, but he was too heavy. As his paws squirmed for hold, the earth gave way. As though in desperation, the badger fixed his eyes on Notail. Softly, Hardclaw extended a claw. In a desperate attempt to get assistance, Notail thought of calling. No. Intent on make one last push.

The badger moaned, "My rats," before disappearing underground. As he hit the ground, he said, "My rats!" Like a fading memory, his voice trailed off.

Bone recoiled from the precipice. The puppy's hind legs were shaking.

Notail said, "He is gone."

The pup beamed a happy face. Laughed Notail.

You found me," Bone said as they returned to the tree line. "Of course, you would,"

I should have never left you," Notail murmured, but Bone was preoccupied.

The puppy was looking up at the stars. Constant showers of stars pounded the night sky, leaving behind a trail of crimson light on the horizon.

When the stars fall ceased, they continued westward at a leisurely pace. Always looking to the west.

Chapter 19: This is the story of a father, and it's

It felt like the night would never end. It seemed like the moor went on forever. The western horizon seemed inaccessible and far.

As they walked along, Bone wondered aloud, "Where does the sun go?"

The notail grins. He hadn't felt that shoulder soreness in a while. He tried to block off all thoughts of Hardclaw. It's a weird and wonderful world, he told himself. The Manless Land sprang to mind. As a fox, he would be familiar with the territory.

Into the west, he proclaimed.

Bone froze, then turned his head to gaze in both directions.

The puppy enquired, "Which direction is west?"

Notail's head was tilted. That's how he put it. "In the direction, we're headed."

And the Manless Land is the same?" Bone remarked.

Notail acknowledged with a nod and continued. A secure location to sleep was essential. It was becoming so cold that his nose was starting to freeze. Having no nose and no tail was not something he was fond of contemplating.

Bone inquired, "Who is the Pale Fox?"

Snowflakes started to fall. A relaxed and slow-motion drift.

He's the grandpa of foxes, Notail said. The Pale Fox was a figure from his father's tales, and he recalled them fondly. Legends that have been told by foxes to foxes ever since they first began hunting in the Manless Land.

As he brushed the snow from his ears, he thought, "I will never tell my cubs the tale."

Saying, "I could tell you the tale if you want, the one my father told me," Notail offered his services.

It seems like Bone perked up his ears.

The snow began to accumulate. Notail recounted Bone the same tale his father had told him as they walked on across the endless moor. It was a tale he should have shared with his cubs.

Notail started by saying that once upon a time when there were no humans, the first fox awakened. His skin was as white as the snow falling outside. When he woke up, he saw gold flecks in his eyes and heard Mother Vixen's voice.

A Pale Fox, she referred to him as. Please go and wake up my kids, you pale fox."

And so it was that the Pale Fox, wandering the world's forest, went from den to den rousing the slumbering foxes. Once he was finished, Mother Vixen beckoned to him once again.

She pleaded with the Pale Fox to "Pale Fox" her children.

Nothing could make the Pale Fox stop laughing.

He enquired, "From what shall I protect them?" Your offspring are the world's quickest, most perceptive, and smartest creatures. They are immune to every danger.

Mother Vixen's tone, however, hardened. Lightning and thunder followed. A storm was beginning to stir.

'Pale Fox,' she referred to him as. "Pale Fox, the man is on his way."

The Pale Fox felt a shiver go through her at the sound of the name. In any case, he was not on good terms with Man, even if he had no idea what the term meant.

I will protect your children from man, he assured Mother Vixen.

The fox mother approved.

As the rain gently patted his fur, the Pale Fox bent his head. After a while, Mankind became aware of his surroundings, and shortly after, Man sought to claim the whole planet for himself. As a result, trees crashed to the ground. With its size reduced, the woodland disappeared. The caverns were stuffed full. The whole world shifted.

As the Pale Fox called out, the foxes arrived.

They turned to Pale Fox and said, "What will we do?" Westward, guided by the Pale Fox. They chased the fading light of the sun. In the end, they reached uncharted woodland on gentle slopes that had never seen human feet.

Announcing that "this land shall be our territory," the Pale Fox made it clear that they intended to make it their own. "The Land Where No Men Live"

So it turned out. Although humanity conquered the globe, the Manless Land was uninhabited for a considerable amount of time. On the other hand, some foxes had an insatiable appetite. They strolled up to the frontier of the Manless Land and took a deep breath of the fresh air. They could smell all the manmade foods, fire-altered meats, and man-made waste products. The first stone forest was wafting its aromas their way.

They said, "We could eat well out there." As the saying goes, "We could hunt well."

With a shake of his head, the Pale Fox dismissed the idea.

A firm "no" came from his mouth as he addressed the foxes. These are your lands. You may join the realm of men if you leave now. There, I won't be able to shield you.

But the foxes were ravenously hungry thanks to the human meal aromas wafting through the stone forest. They were enticed by the stone forest glow. They want more. When the Pale Fox tried to stop them, they just departed the Manless Land. An elderly fox, the eldest of the foxes in the Manless Land, was the very last to go. Both he and his cubs were skilled hunters.

Old Fox, the Pale Fox referred to himself as. Know that I shall always be hunting in the west, in the Manless Land, when you get weary of the world of men. Let your folks know that I am ready to welcome them back at any time. Warn them that their Manless Land will never be populated again. Remember Old Fox, you are wild and cannot be tamed by man, you are wild and this is your land."

The Old Fox accepted the Pale Fox's words and repeated them to his cubs who taught them to their cubs and soon all foxes everywhere understood that despite they had abandoned the Manless Land it would never dwindle, it would never depart this planet. To recall this, we need just see the setting sun in the west. Out there, someplace, is a home where no man can hurt us, where we will never go hungry, where the Pale Fox will honor his vow to Mother Vixen and protect her cubs."

At last, they arrived at the moor's end. They could see groups of trees up ahead. What was beyond those trees were hidden by the darkness, but there was a peculiar rustling in the air.

Bone inquired whether there were any stray canines around.

Notail mused, "Perhaps once." Maybe there are a few left, but all the dogs I've ever met have been obedient to their human masters. Up till you."

The two of them tuned in to the muttering. It seems to have originated outside the forest's boundary. This noise was familiar to Notail, but he couldn't place it. The water. To the west lay the ocean. Always looking to the west.

Bone expressed his desire to "live the life of a wild dog" by saying so.

Notail said, "Take a look around." "There is no man in this place. Being man-free has given you your wild nature. Now, Bone, you have become a wolf dog.

Bone cast his gaze westward.

The Black Dog and I are indeed both canines, he continued. What's to stop it from accompanying you into the Manless Land if I can do so? What if it follows us and harms us?

When Notail gazed westward, he went too far. He had previously said that dogs belonged in the Land of Man and that the Manless Land was more suited to foxes. However, he was unable to provide any absolutes on this matter. He was hesitant to make this admission. For Notail, it was enough that Bone expressed interest in joining him. The fact that Bone was wild was sufficient.

It won't come with us," Notail assured us. To paraphrase, "It can't harm us if we make it to the Manless Land. We are the wild, he is tame. At the end of the day, it is all that counts.

Chapter 20: Getting Out of the Never Can Be Forest

When his father was very old and Mama Vixen was calling him, he remarked, "The melody of the west is the sound of the sea." When the remarks were first spoken to Notail, he ignored them. The idea that he may have to uproot his life and go out west, away from his family and friends, had never occurred to him. As a tribute to the sea anthem sung by his dad.

After a long day of exploring, Bone attempted to find a comfortable sleeping spot under fallen ash, but Notail admonished the pup to instead remain on his feet.

He remarked, "We have job to do before we sleep."

Bone admired the twisted ash branches with desire. Notail yawned, exhausted like the little dog, and he too glanced up to the branches, where they would be protected from the night's chill and where a comfortable bed of pulped leaves awaited them. The snow had dropped, leaving a clean blanket all around them, but there was still work to be done.

Bone was instructed to "walk ahead of me." Simply go in a straight line unless I tell you otherwise.

They had a long trek ahead of them. Their prints in the snow were clear and distinct. Every once in a while Bone would look back at Notail with eyes that implored him to tell him it was time to rest, but all Notail would do was shake his head.

Finally, they reached the main track. There was silence and emptiness there now in the night, but the snow had been crushed by men carriers into icy gullies. Outside of it, Notail could more plainly hear the ocean.

Notail said, "We may go back to sleep now."

“Back?” remarked Bone. Can't we just take a break here?

Notail shook his head once again.

To recapitulate: "We go back," he said. Let's circle back to the tree that crashed down. Right back where we started."

After irritably scraping the cold main track, Bone finally questioned, "Then why have we come here?"

This main track would allow us to cover a lot of ground with very little trace left behind by our paws. Will we?" Bone said eagerly.

With a grin on his face, Notail grinned.
False, since Notail quickly responded. "Neither right now nor tomorrow."

With a shrug, Bone turned around, but Notail held him back.

He then added, "And we go back precisely the way we came." We leave as discreetly as possible. We never stray from the path blazed before us.

Even though Bone did not seem to be persuaded, he followed Notail anyhow, being as cautious as he could be in his pawprints.

When they reached the little wood, Bone made a beeline for the ground under the fallen ash.

Notail relaxed on the plush lives next to him, waiting for Bone to ask him one of his inquiries. Every night, one last query would keep one up.

If I don't have a guy to take care of me, will I have to? enquired Bone.

False, since Notail quickly responded. Now you have become a savage dog.

Closed his eyes and murmured, "Good, I'm weary of man," Bone remarked. I'm going to the Manless Land and living like a wolf.

A nap was for Noatil.

In his sleep, he dreamt.

It was summertime and he was in a verdant forest above gentle slopes. The snow was soft and melting quickly. The heat from his body had reached his paws. They were green on the branches, and they wouldn't ever fall.

As expected, the White Fox showed up. In appearance, he matched Notail's expectations. As pristine and white as the snow that the Manless Land had discarded, with golden glints in its eyes.

The Pale Fox said, "You found me, Notail," before bolting into the woods and racing away. The owl yowled. As soon as Notail saw the Pale Fox, he took off after it.

They continued to run for many days. At other times, they were side by side, and sometimes one would go ahead of the other. There was no evidence that humans existed. Around them, greenery exploded in every direction. Just a never-ending wood. Imagine a planet that never ends and keeps growing. Grass, moss, ferns, and trees are all unencumbered by the drab grey that dominates the human sphere. Soft sunlight penetrated the tree canopy. With its illumination, it created a masterpiece. It resulted in a world that was always alert, which never became weary or grew in darkness. Running didn't tire him out at all. In a sense, the ground under his feet carried him as he raced. No matter how long he ran, he would never tire.

When the Pale Fox finally slowed down, they were standing in a green clearing in the middle of the forest.

Foxes, in Notail's opinion, were everywhere.

He recognized these foxes as ones he had met before. His parents were there, of course. It was there that he discovered Hunter dozing down behind a tree. There was his companion there. While his two pups slept, he nuzzled them to comfort them.

His partner said gently, "Don't wake them," and he nuzzled at her. They snored for a long time.

His mother stared at him in the same wonderment she had always shown: amazement that he was still alive, and determination that he had not given up.

The west, his father assured him, was not far away.

Notail surveyed the open area in search of the Pale Fox, but could not see him. Only the foxes he was familiar with were present.

The question, "Where is the Pale Fox?" Notail inquired.

They all ignored him.

As soon as they woke up, his cubs went to him. He snuffled affectionately at them. He sat back and observed as they engaged in play.

His partner questioned if he intended to make this his permanent residence.

Her words came out in a low whisper, like the sound of the ocean. She was speaking so softly that he hardly registered it.

His mouth formed the word "yes," but no sound came out.

With time, the clearing disappeared. There was a gradual fading away of the foxes he had known all his life. The White Fox had reappeared.

The Pale Fox awoke and murmured, "You should arise now," its golden eyes twinkling.

At that moment, Notail felt a paw jabbing at him. Upon opening his eyes, he saw Bone.

Bone spoke with trembling terror and awe, "It was here." What happened was that it completely bypassed us. However, it followed our footprints and went right on by.

Time of day: morning. Big paw tracks could be seen in the snow throughout the woods. Only the wind wailing through the trees could be heard. There was a chuckle from Notail.

He said, "We fooled it," his shortened tail wagging like a cub's. The two of us managed to outsmart it, Bone. We fooled him.

Bone scowled as he saw the footprints in the snow.

From the shadows of the fallen ash, Notail rushed, darting this way and that across the clearing until his paw prints had erased the Black Dog. The possibility of escaping the Black Dog and making it to the Manless Land. It's a trick, he told himself almost in astonishment, and I've been a part of the deception.

Chapter 21: Insights from the Godwit

They left the little group of trees and followed the sea's lullaby to the beach. Everywhere you looked, all you saw was water. He looked out at the ocean's endless blue and realized that this must be where all water eventually ends up. Clean, fresh air mingled with its abundance of it. It roused him, filling his lungs to the point that he wanted to dash down to the shore and dive headfirst into the ocean. The dunes had a little dusting of snow, but the beach was golden and covered with all sorts of shells. The coast was littered with bladderwrack, and hermit crabs darted silently between the rock pools.

The dune gave way, and Bone rolled down to the sand below. At the next bend on the beach, seals were sunbathing on the rocks just below a chalk cliff. Several seabirds landed on the rock wall. The waves only produced a faint sound as they lapped at the cliff and beach, but the seabirds were noisy as they squawked and called to one another.

While Notail pawed at a crab, Bone crunched on some bladderwrack.

Tiny pieces of bladderwrack were lodged between the puppy's teeth, and he wondered whether they were safe to consume.
The fox shook his head.

Not them, he emphasized. Perhaps there are fish, however.

The shoreline curved into a crescent. On the eastern side were the white chalk cliffs, while the western side had gentler dunes. West is always the direction we go.

They took a stroll out into the shallows and gazed into the azure sea. It completely encased their paws.

Cold, Bone remarked. "That's what I call good!"

There were a lot more shells and fewer, smaller crabs, but no fish came to swim around their claws.

Is there anything being done for them?" Bone questioned, pointing to the birds of the water.

Notail's eyes swept the cliffs. The shrill cries of the seagulls clashed with the sea's acoustics. This was an already chaotic situation that he did not want to further. A lone godwit was perched nearby, observing them.

Notail said, "Birds know the earth."

Bone followed him as he sprang over the dunes to the godwit.
The godwit remained still. Its eyes were fixed on the ocean beyond them. Its very dark eyes appeared to be fixed on something in the ocean's depths. Its large, pointed beak could smash through sand and pierce the surface of the ocean. It strutted confidently, holding its rounded head high. Its feathers mirrored the beach, with their flecks of yellow and brown representing the sand after the tide had receded. When it finally faced them, it blinked its beady eyes and stared down its slick beak.

Is this the Wild West? Asked Notail.

A tilted head was all the godwit could manage.

It said, "Yes if you're traveling west."

The notail nuzzled in. No flight was made by the bird.

Do you know who the Pale Fox is?" Notail probed.

The godwit turned its head back toward the water. There wasn't any turbulence in the water. The season of winter was ending. A gentle wind from the north felt pleasant and comforting. The seagulls raised their cries.

The godwit said, "I have heard of him."

The godwit continued to stare further into the distance. Notail pondered what it might be hunting for in space.
The godwit looked momentarily at Notail before turning back to the ocean, as if to say, "You won't find all your answers in your west." I recognize your needs. Man-free territory. Enjoy some tranquility and downtime. A beacon of hope. We're all guilty of wanting such things so much that we lose sight of our immediate surroundings. "We lose sight of what's important.

There is a place called The Manless Land, Notail cut in. There is such a thing as "The Pale Fox."

There was a nod from the godwit.

The godwit said that if you think they do, they must be real. It looked at Bone once, as though observing the pup for the first time. I don't buy it, therefore it must not be real. There is a way to get there. I've given all hope of ever tracking it down. I'll come up with a solution. You won't ever be able to locate it.

If you don't think it's out there, how can you say for sure that I won't discover it? expressed Notail, who was perplexed.

The godwit looked back toward the horizon and murmured, "We lose what is real...and cling to what just exists."
Notail scratched his paw on the sand. Strange words came out of the bird's mouth. As a whole, he found them distasteful.

"How in the world did you hear about the Pale Fox?" questioned Notail.

The godwit temporarily shut its eyes. It did not turn its head to look at Notail when it opened them.

Finally, it continued, "Others like you have arrived."

The Pale Fox and other foxes arrived here, you say? declared Notail.

There was a nod from the godwit. The gull flew above. In other words, it wept. The godwit glanced at it before returning his gaze to the ocean.

I know a grey fox," the godwit remarked. She spends day and night scouring the dunes for food. It's Wanderer that she goes by. Perhaps she has the coordinates for your Pale Fox and can help you find it.

Notail finally broke his silence and murmured, "Thank you."

The godwit stared at him intently.

The bird questioned, "Why do you thank me?" Listen to me, you fox without a tail: there are solutions to every problem, but they may not be the ones you assume. Before you pose a question, give it some serious consideration. You can't go west, since the west is here, there, east, everywhere, and beyond.

After tapping its beak twice on the rock, the godwit flew off in the direction of the water.

Notail peered westward at the dune field that was covered with snow.

Chapter 22: Four Fox Lengths and Not One Inch Closer

As the tide started to come in, they ascended the dunes. The tall grass pushed against the bleached sand, trying to free itself. In a depression in the dunes, the grey fox rested on the sand that had covered a man's track.

She had lost a lot of weight to the point that patches of red flesh showed through her sparse fur. She rubbed her ear with a paw. Notail hung back. The mangy wasn't the first time he'd seen it. Stay four fox lengths away from the mangy, his father had always warned him. Can't go any farther away from that. And you should never put your faith in them.

Notail questioned, "Are you, Wanderer?"

The fox, grey in color, nodded.

She said softly, "I'm named that." While not by my mom.

Her focus went to the remaining portion of Notail's tail. She gave him a warm grin as she saw him.

She guessed roughly at her name and stated as much.

Notail snarled and flashed his fangs. Her grin slowly vanished.

He replied, "You don't need to know my name." He saw her tattered coat of fur. That striking shade of crimson. what felt like death clinging to her. The godwit said you are familiar with the area; please tell me whether he was correct.

The grey fox looked downcast. Her eyes were shut for a brief second. Notail, his jaw still set and his fangs showing, thought, "She's thinking about what she can gain out of this."

She opened her eyes and said, "I do know this country." The redness and moisture of their skin were striking. This illness had weighed her down so much.

She got to her feet and did some stretching. Painful bony protrusions from her rib cage dug into her exposed skin.

'I am seeking the Pale Fox and the Manless Land,' Notail said her.

Bone reached out to go closer, but Notail blocked his path.

He then hushed Bone, telling him to keep his distance.

Wanderer's pupils contracted.

Yes, she answered. You should keep your distance from me, dog; I may have a human hidden in my tail.

She probed to the tail's end. Bone was the focus of her gaze as she sighed. Notail realized she had made a decision, but he couldn't tell what it was by gazing into her eyes.

The Pale Fox is someone she knows, and she offered to introduce you to her. There was an alteration in her voice. It lost whatever sensitivity it may have had and replaced it with poison. She refused to look Notail in the eye.

Bone had withdrawn to where Notail was standing, and she cast a glance his way.

Although you'll have to stick with me. Naturally, from a safe distance.

She broke towards the dunes and dashed into them. Bone gave a hopeful glance at Notail, and the latter nodded in response. When the dunes ended and the swamp began, they followed her there. The ocean was always nearby. Seagulls' cries and the sound of waves crashing on the coast were constants. As they went by a field, they heard a lamb bleating as a guy dug in the snow to retrieve it. Above them, gulls shouted out inaudible syllables that Notail could not decipher. There was no sign of distress on the grey fox's face, and it kept on racing without uttering a sound.

When they reached a creek, they followed it west, west, and west some more until they came across a massive wooden manden that was completely isolated from any other maidens in the area.

Notail, curious, inquired, "What is this place?" as they lay outside the manden. "Where is the White Fox?"

A glance from the grey fox below.

"You told me to bring you here," she said. The Pale Fox will track you down to this area.

A door at one end of the mandate allowed for easy access. Notail peered inside and saw that it was littered with dried, brittle grass. Those maidens of the stone forest have nothing on this.

Notail hesitated when Wanderer padded inside. He took a survey of the rapidly defrosting environment. Through the relentless white, he could make out a sliver of green. He felt certain that his trip was almost over. He was now in the western hemisphere. You knew that Man's Land couldn't be too far away. Still, it wasn't right. The presence of man here is explicable. The Pale Fox, according to the myths, has always lived in a remote, uninhabited area. This area reeked of man and his cherished possessions.

And yet, he was in the west now.

What should we do now? Bone enquired, wagging his tail.

Notail glanced at the manden. Human aromas poured out in abundance.

He then instructed them to follow the grey fox inside, saying simply, "We follow her."

Chapter 23: Within the Dark and the Light

The sunset rapidly, and nighttime came early. Large striped spiders were the only apparent inhabitants of the manden, which consisted only of dark crevices and nooks where they spun webs. As nightfall approached, more and more of them emerged.

As the grass died, Notail paced back and forth over it. The Pale Fox will be here soon, he knew.

In contrast to the grey fox, who snuggled up tightly for sleep, Bone kept a wary watch on the spiders.

How long till the Pale Fox appears? Asked Notail.

Have patience. She turned her back on Notail and whispered, "I assure you, he will arrive."

The odor of misplaced items permeated the area. Everything around Notail warned him to flee. To go. But he continued to wait there anyway.

He persuaded himself, "I've arrived to the west; the Pale Fox will come."

That confidence is what kept him there.

Is it a common occurrence for you to hang out with the Pale Fox? The question was posed by NoTail.

With a grin on her face, she continued. Now when she smiled, he found himself disliking her eyes.

She responded, "Many times," but her voice sounded distant and sluggish. This fox has "met him more than any other fox."

Notail saw her flushed face and emaciated limbs. The myth states that the Pale Fox will accept any foxes into his home. Do wild foxes like this one fall within that category?

You're scratching your head, she said, wondering whether you believe me. What I hear you saying is, "You're wondering whether the Pale Fox would reveal himself to a fox like me.

Notail was unable to respond. Her gaze traveled to the tip of his tail and back.

I get it," she murmured, getting to her feet and coming closer to him. As usual, her grin was a little tense. Many foxes likely share your opinion. On the other hand, Notail? Do I have the right name for you?

No tailing nod. He turned his head aside and said nothing.
He finally managed to get out an "I'm sorry," his voice cracking slightly.

When he looked behind him, the grey fox met his gaze.

Therefore, I am as well. Unfortunately, that opportunity has passed. The Pale Fox was someone you hoped to meet. 'Well, now you finally do.

The moon's weak illumination gradually faded. Darker than the darkness, much larger, and reeking of human sweat and body odor, he beheld the black figure.

With a snort and a wide maw, the Black Dog threatened. Its salivary glands were dripping and its teeth were shining. Its crimson, moist tongue kissed its teeth. In a word, it was massive. Much bigger than the canine residents of the stone forest, where Notail grew up, had ever seen before. Even more robust. It had rippling muscles throughout its body. It was producing some kind of heat. The last gasp of life. The inhalation of flaming air. Human breathe with all the stench it brings.

It was Notail's roar that jolted Bone awake. The puppy raised its anxious little head and moaned.

Somehow, the Black Dog managed to have his voice heard.

I find you fox, he said, his words dripping with the might of his whole gigantic physique. "I…end…you."

Barking so loudly that it rocked the manden, the Black Dog scared the striped spiders back into their burrows.

Notail was the target.

Despite knowing it was a lost cause, Notail leaped toward the shadow that had been following him for so long.

He told himself, "I will make this end" as he stood up to face the Black Dog's bared teeth.

Chapter 24: There Is No End To A Story

Notail's muzzle was ripped off by ripping claws.

After Notail let out a cry, the two of them landed in the dead grass, where the Black Dog instantly sprang on top of Notail and began chewing at his leg.

Black Dog barked, "You...nothing," as Notail fought to get to his feet.

Notail tried to hurt the Black Dog by kicking it with his paws, but he was unsuccessful. Despite the Black Dog's apparent indifference to Notail's frantic punches, the latter's fur was stained red by the latter's repeated bites.

The words "I am nothing" came out of Notail's feeble mouth. As the fox, I am.

A chuckle came from the direction of the Black Dog.

Notail screamed and fell on the floor.

He heard Bone raise a snarl and watched his companion take a stride toward him before he passed

out from the agony. The Black Dog's bloody face looked up at Bone the moment he moved.
It spat, "Stay...dog."

Closer and closer did the Black Dog slink toward Bone. Bloody maws yawned at the puppy.

The bone remained immobile.

The Black Dog commanded, "Heel...dog," and as if under the influence of a hypnotic trance, Bone padded over and sat down in front of the Black Dog.

The message read, "You, are you for man?"

Bone was dwarfed by the Black Dog's height. The animal's mouth widened. The animal brushed its tongue over its teeth.

There was no retreat from Bone.

Notail's pulse quickened as the puppy opened his jaws to respond. He saw that Bone was hopeless. After he spoke what Notail expected him to say, the Black Dog would kill him instantly. The ache in his whole body prevented Notail from getting to his feet.

“Who your master dog?” the Black Dog remarked.

Bone boldly said, "I have no master," his voice wavering but yet mustering a roar. Only my pal is with me.

It hissed, "You finish now." The creature's body floated down toward Bone. Its jaws closed on Bone's neck, lifting him into the air and shaking him in all directions. Bone howled in agony and flailed his legs, but his struggle ceased swiftly and he hung there limply in the Black Dog's jaws, the crimson fangs digging deep into Bone's fur.

Notail's voice was faint and fading as he shouted out, "Leave him."

Bone was tossed to one side by the Black Dog. The puppy collapsed lifelessly upon the dead grass. How still he was.

The Black Dog's attention refocused on Notail. Notail peered beyond it to Bone as it approached after the little dog, and he kept looking until he noticed the tiniest of breaths. The puppy was still fighting. Bone peeled his eyelids wide. His eyes glowed with vitality. They made a plea for aid. They looked directly at Notail and summoned him.

Notail's eyes landed on Bone. He hadn't even grown up yet; he was only a pup. Even a cub.

Notail was having second thoughts. No more of it!

He mustered every ounce of strength he had left, opened his jaws wide, sprang, and sank his teeth deeply into the Black Dog's neck. He hastily yanked aside the dark hair and flesh. There was a profuse loss of blood.

The Black Dog made a feeble attempt to scream out, but all that came out was a croak. Suddenly, its eyes were moist. Shaking its head, it stumbled away from Notail. As the Black Dog pawed at its throat, desperately trying to stop the bleeding, Notail forced himself to his feet.

The Black Dog sputtered, "You end me," as blood gushed from its lips.

Notail said, "I am a fox."

Disbelief could be seen in his bloodshot eyes. As the Black Dog collapsed, Notail hobbled over to help.

The blackness morphed into darkness. Darkness becomes darkness. The result was the same as the input: a void.

Chapter 25: Clearing in the Everlasting Woods

Yet Notail realized there was nothing more to do.

Notail murmured, "Help me," and, with one useless leg dragging after him, walked out of the manden while leaning on Bone. He could smell sunrise. He could see dawn breaking. The air contained the fragrances of spring. He could hear the melody of the waves.

When he landed, he felt grass on his fur. Living grass freed free from snow.

Bone attempted to persuade Notail to rise by shoving his snout into his side, but Notail remained seated.

The puppy begged its owner, "Please don't go."

Even Notail cracked a grin sometimes.

“I think,” he replied, “this is where we have to part.”

Don't go there," Bone admonished. The Manless Land and the Pale Fox await us. Together, I know we can get there.

Notail shook his head, and the resulting body creases showed.
"I will not discover the Pale Fox with you, Bone," he murmured, his grin fading. It's become clear to me. That attempt of mine was unsuccessful. There was no point in this journey that I brought you on. I had hoped that we would discover the Manless Land; I had assumed that it was to the west. But now I'm not so sure; I can't see it or feel it.

When Bone was close to Notail, he would rub his head on his chest.

Bone said, "You're mistaken." You were my savior. You showed me how to be wild. Through the snow, you led me. I would have ended without you. We discovered the west, we found it together."

With that, Notail averted his gaze. The puppy's hair was soft and warm on his skin. He is correct, though Notail, I took him west, I kept him alive. I have done that, maybe it is enough.

Leave me, Bone," Notail said quietly. "At the moment, I am content with my situation."

Here, he told himself, there is no longer any need to be afraid. I am now in the western hemisphere.

Bone tried to reassure Notail that this was not the case, telling him that the two of them would eventually track down the Pale Fox and hunt the Manless Land together, that they would remain best friends until old age, and that their barks would be no louder than those of puppies and cubs, but Notail was deaf to his words. Notail was already in the woodland clearing, gazing over his sleeping offspring while cuddling up to his mate under the unflinching light of the sun that never went down.

Epilogue

A new day has begun. It was no longer winter, and the snow had melted. No shadows could be seen. No pollutants were present in the atmosphere.

There were signs of spring wherever you looked, like budding flowers and chirping birds. Finally, springtime! It was a warm day. There was nothing but good about the day.

Take a deep breath, Bone told himself, and head west. Always looking to the west.

www.ingramcontent.com/pod-product-compliance
Lightning Source LLC
LaVergne TN
LVHW012102160826
845678LV00014B/2910